# METHODS AND MATERIALS FOR CONDUCTING

# METHODS AND MATERIALS FOR CONDUCTING

DOUGLAS STOTTER

GIA Publications, Inc.
Chicago

G-6736
Copyright © 2006
GIA Publications, Inc.
7404 South Mason Avenue, Chicago 60638

Cover design: Nikki Wilkens

ISBN: 1-57999-551-9

Printed in the United States of America

# CONTENTS

## Part 2: Excerpts

## PART 3: INSTRUCTOR GUIDE

# Preface—About This Text

This text has been designed to meet several goals:

- to provide an easy-to-follow, systematic, and progressive manual of physical technique
- to provide a wide variety of musical excerpts of varying length and complexity with special attention to wind band literature
- to provide these materials in such a way as to allow for maximum flexibility and usefulness in course structure and content

The majority of excerpts are taken from standard and classic band literature. This way, the conducting student and future wind band conductor can begin his or her familiarization with the content and challenges of this literature at the start of conducting training. These excerpts will also aid string players/conductors (especially music education majors) by increasing their familiarity with the music and composers of high-quality wind band music.

For a more detailed description of how this textbook can be used in beginning through advanced conducting classes, see the Instructor Guide starting on page 223.

# ACKNOWLEDGMENTS

Specials thanks and appreciation go to Stephen Pratt, Harvey Benstein, and Steven Eggleston, whose suggestions and encouragement have been invaluable in the creation of this text.

Learning to conduct and to teach conducting is a lifelong journey I have not yet completed. I gratefully acknowledge all of the teachers and colleagues from whom I have learned so much and from whom I continue to learn. From my student days at the University of Michigan, I thank H. Robert Reynolds, Carl St. Clair, Jerry Junkin, Larry Rachleff, Eric Becher, and Elizabeth A. H. Green; from the University of Iowa, Myron Welch and James Dixon; and from my years in the Band Department of Indiana University, Ray Cramer, Stephen Pratt, and David Woodley. I would also like to express my gratitude to those "along the way" who shared their expertise in summer conducting workshops around the country: Craig Kirchhoff, Stanley DeRusha, Allan McMurray, and many others.

I would like to thank the people at GIA Publications who made this book possible and assisted in its editing, design, and publication: Elizabeth Bentley, Martha Chlipala, Alec Harris, Robert Sacha, and Linda Vickers.

Teachers learn as much from their students as their students learn from them. Special thanks go to twenty years of students who have taught me to be a better conductor, musician, and human being.

# PART 1:
## MANUAL OF TECHNIQUE

# Unit 1
# On the Podium

## Posture and Stance

Establishing a proper stance and posture on the podium is the crucial first step for the beginning conductor. A proper position for the legs and feet:

- will be comfortable and easily maintained over long periods on the podium
- will establish a neutral and natural appearance
- will help prevent extraneous side-to-side and front-to-back movement that could draw attention away from the ictus and make it difficult to focus on beat pattern and gesture

A proper position for arms and hands:

- will be comfortable and easily maintained over long periods
- will establish a neutral and natural appearance
- will enable players to focus simultaneously on the baton and the conductor's face

Positions of the hands and feet depend on body type and build. Strive for a relaxed position. Follow these steps to establish a personal conducting position:

1. Take several steps forward and stop with feet parallel. Observe the distance between the feet. This is a natural distance; spacing much different from this may cause excessive swaying or lack of balance.

2. Put equal weight on both feet and spread that weight evenly from heel to toe. Uneven weight distribution is another major cause of one of the novice conductor's worst enemies: swaying.

3. Rest your arms comfortably at your sides. Relax the lower body, and do not lock the knees. Feel the ground in the soles of your feet; feel the weight of the body in the pelvis. This grounded state will contribute to stability and help to maintain an upright posture with a straight but relaxed back.

When a relaxed and natural lower body position is achieved, only then should you proceed to the next steps, which place your arms and hands in the proper ready position. Correct arm and hand placement are the first keys to successful communication between conductor and player—this cannot be overemphasized.

1. Raise your right arm as if to shake someone's hand. The shoulder should be no higher than it is when your arm is at your side. The upper arm should not contact any part of the torso. The elbow should be IN FRONT of the body and to the side with a comfortable bend. The lower arm should angle up from the elbow so as to be beyond parallel with the ground as well as angle slightly in toward the center of the body.

2. Turn your wrist just inward and drop the hand slightly. Stop just BEFORE your palm is parallel to the ground. Keep all fingers together and your hand and wrist relaxed.

3. Raise the left arm to mirror the right. This is a natural READY POSITION. When the baton is added to the right hand, the conductor is in a position to establish player eye contact with the baton in view.

## CHOOSING A BATON

Choosing a baton is more than a personal matter of comfort or style. It is important to select a baton that does more than simply look and feel good. A baton must also fit the hand in such a way as to allow for a grip that:

- can be maintained over a long period without fatigue
- allows for flexibility in fingers and wrist
- allows the baton to be held with index finger and thumb at the balance point
- allows the shaft of the baton to exit the hand in the proper direction
- allows for control of the baton with the second, third, and possibly fourth fingers of the hand

Baton handles are usually pear-shaped, straight, or straight with a slight taper. The shape and size of your hand and fingers determine which of these shapes best fulfills the qualifications above.

The best length for your baton is based on the size of your forearm. Baton length will appear most natural for you if the length of the shaft approximately equals that of your forearm. Try this test:

1. Place the baton in your hand with the handle in your palm or fingers at the point you would grip the baton.

2. Lay the baton handle along the back of your forearm toward the back of your elbow.

3. A baton that reaches the inside bend of the elbow without passing it is most likely to look natural for your body size.

Most batons are made of wood, either left natural or painted white, or are made of fiberglass, usually an off-white color. Although fiberglass batons are less likely to warp or break, their somewhat blue tinge makes them difficult to see, especially in fluorescent light. The choice of natural color or white for a wood baton should be based on the conducting environment—do not use a white baton if conducting against a white backdrop; do not use a brown/natural baton if your backdrop is close to that color.

## Holding the Baton

The baton grip should be firm and secure. Ensure that:

- the wrist and fingers remain relaxed and flexible, allowing for a full range of motion
- the baton-hand combination presents only one point of focus (the baton tip)
- the tip of the baton remains within an imaginary line drawn from the conductor's to the player's eyes (the communication line)

Follow these steps for a proper baton grip:

1. Grip the baton lightly at its balance point between the thumb and the first joint of the forefinger.

2. Bend the thumb with the knuckle slightly outward.

3. Wrap the remaining fingers down and around the baton handle such that the fingertips come in contact with the palm *without squeezing*.

The size and shape of the baton handle should be determined in large part by the size of the hand. If the grip described above cannot be achieved comfortably and securely with a particular handle, try another. Very often the conductor cannot achieve the proper grip while maintaining thumb and forefinger contact at the balance point of the baton. Again, another baton may solve this problem.

The length of the baton should be such that with the proper grip or arm and hand position the tip of the baton is placed between the conductor's eyes and those of the players. This is the all-important communication line. Placing the beat pattern in or near this line is the most efficient method of communicating musical gestures to an ensemble. The communication line is maintained through:

- proper arm and hand position
- proper grip with a baton of proper length
- proper ictus placement

With the baton now held in the right hand, repeat the six steps establishing proper body, arm, and hand position. Imagine an ensemble seated in front of you and check: *Is the tip of the baton in the communication line?*

The tip of the baton must lie in an imaginary line drawn between your eyes and the eyes of your ensemble players. If this is not the case, check your arm and hand position. To raise the baton, move the upper arm and elbow forward (away) from your torso. To move the baton tip closer to the centerline of your body, rotate the wrist.

## MAINTAINING STRAIGHT-LINE MOVEMENT

Human beings were not designed to be good communicators with the baton. Our physiology causes our bodies to move in circular paths, but circular paths do not present equally clear and visible lines of communication to all members of an ensemble. All joint, or hinge, movements describe an arc—part of a circle. Communication between player and conductor is much more efficient if the arm can move in straight lines, not curves. The proper combined use of the body's hinges—fingers, wrist, elbow, and shoulder—will create straight-line movement. Straight-line arm movement will ensure that beat patterns remain in horizontal and vertical planes, which allow for maximum visibility by all players, regardless of their position in the ensemble.

Consider how the combined movement of your hinges can create straight-line arm movement. Left and right arm movement must use the shoulder *and* the elbow. If the right elbow does not open as the right arm moves toward the right, a circular motion (around the shoulder hinge) is created, taking the baton tip out of the horizontal plane most visible to the players.

**EXERCISE 1.1.** Left and Right Arm Movement
- Place both hands in the READY POSITION with palms facing the floor.
- Slowly move both hands out, then back to ready, at all times keeping the hands parallel to the floor with palms down. The hands should move along a straight line; do not curve around the body.
- Allow the wrists to move as well with the fingers pointing more inward while the hands move out and with the fingers pointing outward when hands move in.

Up and down arm movement must use the shoulder, elbow, *and* wrist in order to create straight-line vertical movement. If any one hinge is locked, circular motion results. Circular motion takes the baton out of the area most visible to the players.

**EXERCISE 1.2.** Up and Down Arm Movement
- Place both hands in the READY POSITION with palms facing the floor.
- Slowly move both hands up then back to ready, at all times keeping the hands parallel to each other. The hands should move in a straight line, perpendicular to the floor at all times.
- Be sure that the wrists move as well, keeping the palms facing the floor at all times.

Practice these exercises close to a wall or other vertical, flat surface. As the arms move right and left or up and down, the fingers should remain in contact with the wall at all times.

For a test of relaxed and flexible wrist movement, place a coin on the back of your hand: *it should not fall off as the wrist moves!*

Practice these horizontal and vertical movements until they feel natural. Use a full range of motion while maintaining steady speed with smooth transitions in direction changes. A few minutes of practice each day will help develop straight-line movement that can then be adapted to traditional beat patterns and clearly present the ictus point to the entire ensemble.

## THE ICTUS

The ictus (or beat) point is created by the movement of hinges. Proper hinge movement places the ictus at the tip of the baton. As the novice conductor experiments with arm, wrist, and hand movement, he or she must keep in mind that the ictus is perceived to be at the largest hinge that does not move.

- If the shoulder moves up and down but the elbow does not open and close, the ictus is created at the elbow.
- If the shoulder and elbow move, but the wrist is locked, the wrist (or hand) creates the ictus.
- If the shoulder, elbow, and wrist are flexible, the ictus point is transferred to the tip of the baton.

The novice conductor can practice hinge movement with a simple exercise. It will enable the student to gain control of each hinge, a skill crucial to effective non-verbal communication. A bit of practice each day will ensure that all hinges remain flexible and work in concert to create expressive beat patterns and icti appropriate to the style of the music being conducted.

1. Establish good posture, stance, and arm position. Grip the baton lightly, and ensure that the baton tip is in the communication line.

2. Set a metronome to a moderately slow tempo (e.g., quarter note = 72).

3. Using only your wrist, move the tip of the baton up and down in time creating an ictus with each pulse of the metronome. Maintain a smooth and even movement, being sure to keep your wrist relaxed.

4. Continue creating ictus points, adding elbow movement. Be sure to keep the wrist moving as well! After a time, add shoulder movement. As hinges are added, the ictus point should remain in the same place even as the beat size increases.

5. After reaching a moderately large beat size using all of your hinges, reverse the process. First remove shoulder movement and then elbow movement until only wrist movement remains.

As these movements become more natural, the conductor may want to adapt this exercise for use with various traditional beat patterns. Begin by conducting a 3/4 pattern the size of a postage stamp using only the smallest hinges in the hand. Gradually increase the size of the pattern by adding hinges as explained above. After you gain a moderate level of ease and comfort using the 3/4 pattern, add 4/4 and 2/4 patterns to the drill.

## PREPARATIONS, DOWNBEATS, AND RELEASES

The exercise above is a good first step toward developing preparation and downbeat movements. Be sure to keep the techniques of hinge movement in mind at all times. Preparations at the beginning of pieces must establish:

- the ictus plane
- the dynamic
- the tempo (when to play)
- the style (how to play)

The preparation and first downbeat take as much mental as physical effort. A conductor must have the tempo, dynamic, and style established mentally before making the first move. A good preparation will set the music in motion with the conductor's conception of tempo and style firmly established in the minds of the players. Follow these steps to start the music in motion:

1. Establish your conducting stance with good body, arm, and baton position. Create the communication line and the ictus plane with proper arm and hand position. If conducting with the baton arm alone, place the tip of the baton in line with the center of your body. If mirroring, place each hand equidistant from that centerline.

2. Remain still for a moment to make eye contact with the ensemble.

3. With a slight click or push-off from the ictus plane, move the arm (or arms, if mirroring) straight up, then straight down to the ictus plane as smoothly as possible, ending with another click. Be sure to keep your head up! The time from click or push-off to the return to the ictus plane should equal one beat. Be sure to return to the precise starting point. "Click" the ictus to start the preparation with a quick wrist flick (like striking a match). Push off from the ictus plane with shoulder and elbow movement. Avoid giving beats with your head or knees!

4. A release gesture can look exactly like a preparation because release gestures show similar information. Preparations show when and how to start, and release gestures show when and how to stop.

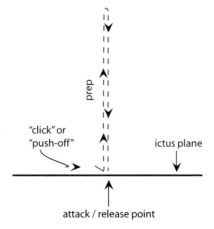

**FIGURE 1.1.** Preparation and Attack/Release

A more emphatic release gesture is accomplished with a circular gesture. Avoid using this type of release for all occasions. The best release gestures remain in the style of the music.

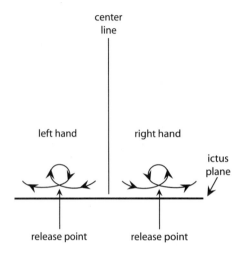

**FIGURE 1.2.** Emphatic Release

Practice giving preparations and release gestures with various tempos, dynamics, and articulations using either one hand or two. Be sure to establish the various musical parameters in your mind before moving.

**EXERCISE 1.3.** Preparations and Releases

*All conducting is preparation.* Every action a conductor wishes to elicit from performers using physical gesture must be prepared. Consider how you would like your players to release a sound, just as you consider how they should start a sound. You must prepare both releases and entrances.

In the first exercise below, determine dynamic and style (articulation) for each note. Prepare and give the entrance with the desired articulation or attack, allow the players to sustain, and then prepare and give a release gesture. Remember, attack and release gestures can look EXACTLY the same. (This exercise can be sung or played.)

For the next exercises, practice entrances with varying tempos, dynamics, and articulations. Use smaller hinges for softer dynamics; only involve larger hinges for louder dynamics. Use the wrist to help indicate articulation; use a relaxed wrist for legato attack and stiffer or quicker wrist movements for a more marcato or accented articulation.

In the staccato exercise, practice the wrist "flick" alone, with no other hinge movement.

Practice each line first with the baton hand alone, then with both hands (mirroring). Do not use beat patterns with these exercises—practice straight up-and-down movements and the use of the wrist to maintain straight-line movement.

In this final exercise, follow the diagram below. Give the preparation and initial attack desired, allow the players to sustain (as arms move out from the centerline), and then give the final emphatic release. Practice with the baton alone, left hand alone (in a mirror image of this diagram), and mirrored with both hands.

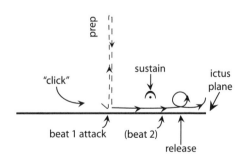

**FIGURE 1.3.** Half Note Fermata with Emphatic Release

# UNIT 2
## CONDUCTING IN THREE, FOUR, TWO, AND ONE

Standing on the podium and beating time does not make one a conductor. However, developing and internalizing basic time-beating skills is the necessary first step to becoming a conductor. The communication of musical ideas must be accompanied by clear beat patterns. In this unit, the beginning student should concentrate on recreating the patterns pictured here with the baton and baton arm. Do not move too quickly to two-handed conducting; the left hand has its own language and should not simply mirror the right unless specific musical communication is intended. The more advanced student can add musical direction as indicated in the excerpts.

### BEAT PLACEMENT AND COMMUNICATION OF STYLE

For each meter, a relative few patterns have evolved over time to become the standards. Conducting students should work to internalize each pattern so they can eventually work on automatic pilot. Relate each pattern to the ictus plane (established by arm and hand position before the preparation) and the centerline. Remember, the ictus plane should be high enough to maintain the visual communication line between conductor and player. When conducting with one hand, the centerline should be close to the center of your body. If you choose to mirror the right-hand pattern in your left hand, move the centerline of each hand's pattern off-center enough to ensure that the right and left hands do not cross.

Pattern clarity is the first goal of time beating. Keep in mind:

- the placement of each beat, specific to meter
- the style of the beat within the continuum from staccato through legato
- the direction of approach to each beat
- the direction of each rebound
- the speed of horizontal movement

For maximum clarity, approach each beat from above the ictus plane and rebound upward and toward the next ictus point. Avoid scooping up to any beat.

In meters with an even number of beats, maintain the symmetry of the pattern. If the distance traveled between beats is not equal, you must adjust the speed of movement so that the time between beats remains constant.

For example, in 4/4 meter the baton must travel twice as far when moving from beat two to three as it does between any other two beats. To maintain a smooth pattern with no hiccups or backbeats, the conductor must double the arm motion speed when moving from two to three as compared with the speed between any other two beats.

Angular patterns show a more marked articulation. As your arms move through these angular motions, the baton (using the wrist) taps each beat slightly, creating a very specific beat point. If the baton motion comes to a point (on the beat), it necessarily stops. This stop indicates the discontinuation of the sound and the more marked articulation. Stopping the baton at the ictus can also show space between the notes. A stopped-beat pattern pauses at each ictus (to show a stop in sound) and then continues along the beat pattern path to prepare the next ictus. The resumption of movement after a stop serves as the preparation for the next event.

To indicate a more legato articulation, avoid coming to a point at the ictus. Do not flick the wrist, but instead ensure that the wrist is relaxed and can move freely. Smooth wrist movement at the ictus helps indicate a smoother articulation. Maintain fluid and continuous motion of the arms to indicate a fluid and continuous sound.

It may be helpful at this early stage of conductor training to make a correlation between baton movement and sound. Think of the baton's movement through the air as a representation of the sound and how it is sustained. Think of how the baton tip strikes the ictus as equivalent to how players might begin a sound. The baton in continuous motion (i.e., with continuous arm motion) indicates a continuation of sound. By using the wrist either actively (e.g., the wrist flick or hand "slap" or "tap" at the ictus) or passively (allowing the wrist to be relaxed enough to move naturally with the momentum of the arms), the conductor can represent attacks from hard and pointed to soft and smooth.

Although this is an oversimplification of how players respond to conductors, this correlation may help novice conductors to conceptualize how they might move the arm, wrist, and baton to describe sound with physical gesture.

## TIME BEATING IN THREE

Start with time beating in three. This pattern concentrates solely on motion on one side of the centerline with the distance between each beat point roughly equal so the speed of the arm movement is constant from beat to beat.

For a marked style, use the wrist with a tapping motion to create a pointed ictus as the arm moves through the pattern with constant motion. For a staccato (separated) style, experiment using the pointed ictus pattern with a stopped beat.

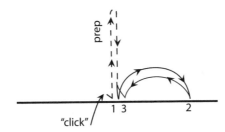

FIGURE 2.1. Pointed Ictus in Three

For a marked style, relax the wrist and let it move up and down naturally with the momentum of the arm. Keep the arm moving with constant motion and speed. Within the constraints of the basic pattern, modify the motion near the beat point to avoid a pointed attack. This will show a more legato articulation.

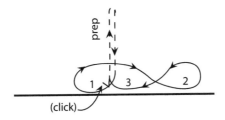

FIGURE 2.2. Legato Ictus in Three

When practicing time beating in three, work to maintain a consistent pattern. Be sure to open the elbow hinge when moving to beat two and close it when moving to beat three. This ensures that the ictus plane is not curved around the body, affording every player a good view of each beat. To begin working on independence of hands, practice each excerpt: (1) right hand alone, (2) left hand alone, and (3) both hands (mirrored).

**EXERCISE 2.1.** Practice in Three

For practice with a pointed ictus and stopped beats:

From *The Italian in Algiers* by Gioachino Rossini. (See page 184 for full version.)

For practice with a legato ictus:

From *Variations on a Korean Folk Song* by John Barnes Chance, copyright © 1967 Boosey & Hawkes, Inc. Used by permission. (See page 86 for full version.)

# TIME BEATING IN FOUR

Time beating in four presents challenges that time beating in three does not—maintaining pattern symmetry and varying speeds of arm movement as the distance between beat points varies. Clarity and precision in the four-beat pattern are maintained by ensuring that the pattern is symmetrical with respect to the centerline. In the diagram below, note that the distance from the centerline to either beat two or three is equal. Also note that the distance between beats two and three is twice the distance between any other two beats. In order to maintain a steady tempo, arm movement must increase in speed proportionally when moving from two to three.

As with time beating in three, work to maintain straight-line body movement through use of shoulder, elbow, and wrist hinges. All beat points should be placed along a straight ictus line—don't let the arm swing around the body:

- When moving toward beat two, reach out to the ictus plane.
- When moving from beat two to beat three, open the elbow.

Practice both staccato and legato styles within the basic four-beat pattern.

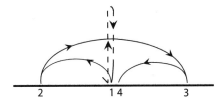

**FIGURE 2.3.**

Pointed Ictus in Four

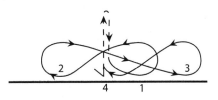

**FIGURE 2.4.**

Legato Ictus in Four

## OTHER FOUR-BEAT PATTERNS

Many other four-beat patterns are acceptable in various situations. Each sacrifices some amount of clarity in favor of other musical or technical benefits. In a focal point pattern, the ictus for each beat is placed in the same location; performers will know exactly where to expect ictus information. This pattern (Figure 2.5), however, can be difficult to follow. The modified four pattern (Figure 2.6) shown here allows for speed though the pattern (there are fewer direction changes) while specific ictus points for beats three and four are more difficult to indicate.

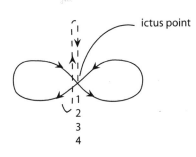

**FIGURE 2.5.**

Focal Point Four-Beat Pattern

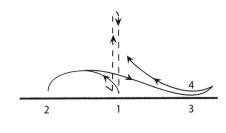

**FIGURE 2.6.**

Modified Movement to Beat Three

**EXERCISE 2.2.** Patterns in Four

Practice with a legato ictus; experiment with varying beat sizes to indicate dynamic changes.

From *Salvation Is Created* by Pavel Tschesnokoff, copyright © 1945 Neil A. Kjos Music Company. Used by permission. (See page 194 for full version.)

Practice in a range of styles from legato to marcato. Use the wrist to move the tip of the baton in the style of articulation desired. Maintain constant arm movement to show a continuation of sound between articulations.

From *Chester* by William Billings. (See page 84 for full version.)

Practice both exercises: (1) right hand alone, (2) left hand alone, and (3) both hands (mirrored).

## TIME BEATING IN TWO

There are many ways of beating time in two-beat measures. Avoid patterns that are too vertical or circular. The amount of movement in the horizontal direction can have a great impact on style in two-beat pieces. Keep in mind, as in all patterns:

- each rebound of the preceding beat is also the preparation for the following beat

Conduct the following excerpt in eight using the four-pattern framework illustrated in Figure 4.3.

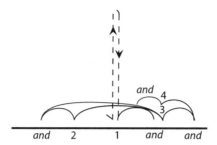

**FIGURE 4.3.** Subdivided Four

From "Pavane" from *William Byrd Suite* by Gordon Jacob
Copyright © 1924 by Boosey & Co. Ltd. Used by permission.
(See page 170 for full version.)

## COMPOUND SUBDIVIDED METERS

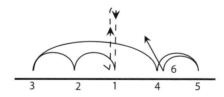

**FIGURE 4.4.** Subdivided Two – Six Beats per Measure

From *The Banks O' Doon* by Robert Burns. (See page 85 for full version.)

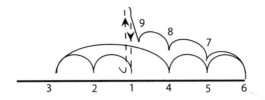

**FIGURE 4.5.** Subdivided Three – Nine Beats per Measure

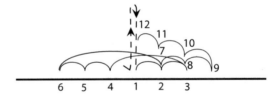

**FIGURE 4.6.** Subdivided Four – Twelve Beats per Measure

## SIMPLE ASYMMETRICAL METERS

Patterns for simple asymmetrical meters such as 5/4 and 7/4 (or 5/8 and 7/8 where eighth notes serve as the pulse) are created in much the same way as divided meters. First, the framework pattern should be determined. This determination can be based on:

- the number of major stresses the measures contains (a 7/4 measure may have three major stresses, on one, three, and six; thus, a three-beat framework of 2 + 3 + 2 beats is used)
- the rhythm of the measure(s)
- the melodic shape of the measure(s)

Following the procedures outlined above for subdividing beats, an asymmetrical pattern is created. In 5/4 meter conducted as 2 + 3, for example, a subdivided two pattern can be used.

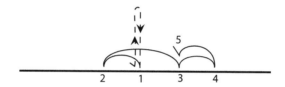

**FIGURE 4.7.** Five Beats (2 + 3)

For a 5/4 measure divided 3 + 2, beats two and three are created by subdividing the first half of the pattern.

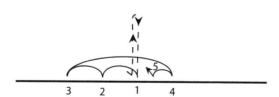

**FIGURE 4.8.** Five Beats (3 + 2)

Using this subdivision method, any simple asymmetrical pattern can be created. 7/4 and 7/8 patterns are based on a three-beat framework; 11/4 is based on a four-beat pattern.

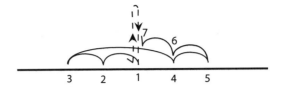

FIGURE 4.9. Subdivided Three – Seven Beats (3 + 2 + 2)

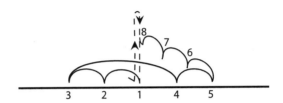

FIGURE 4.10. Subdivided Three – Eight Beats (3 + 2 + 3)

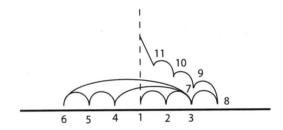

FIGURE 4.11. Subdivided Four – Eleven Beats (3 + 3 + 2 + 3)

## CHANGING METERS

All beat patterns show stresses within the measure. A standard four pattern has a major stress on beat one and a secondary stress on beat three when the pattern crosses over the centerline. Before conducting asummetrical patterns, the conductor must determine the location of any secondary stresses within those measures and choose a pattern that reflects these stresses. For example, in a 5/4 measure, the secondary stress may be on beat three (use a 2 + 3 pattern) or on beat four (use a 3 + 2 pattern).

**EXERCISE 4.3.** Asymmetrical and Changing Meters

For each 5/4 measure, determine if the secondary stress is on beat three (then conduct 2 + 3) or on beat four (then conduct 3 + 2). For each 6/4 measure, determine if there are two main stresses (conduct 3 + 3) or three stresses (conduct 2 + 2 + 2). For practice purposes, conduct a variety of 2 + 3 / 3 + 2 and 2 + 2 + 2 / 3 + 3 in these exercises.

From "Promenade" by Modest P. Mussorgsky. (See page 176 for full version.)

**EXERCISE 4.4.**

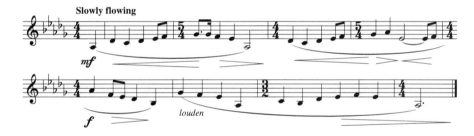

From "Horkstow Grange" by Percy Aldridge Grainger, copyright © 1966 G. Schirmer, Inc. (ASCAP). Used by permission. (See page 94 for full version.)

When changing meters also include measures with different units of pulse, the conductor should work to ensure that the underlying pulse common to all meters remains steady. For example, when 3/8 measures are interspersed among 4/4 or 3/4 measures, the eighth note division of each beat must remain steady. Whether to conduct eighths in such 3/8 measures (rather than one beat to the bar) is determined by tempo. Slower tempos may require beating eighths in 3/8 bars and beating quarters in 4/4 or 3/4 bars.

EXERCISE 4.5.

Conduct 6/8 in two and 3/4 in three.

From "America" by Leonard Bernstein, copyright © 1956, 1957, 1958, 1959 Amberson Holdings LLC and Stephen Sondheim. Used by permission. (See page 83 for full version.)

EXERCISE 4.6.

Conduct each of these lines separately. Practice 3/8 measures in one and three.

From "Lord Melbourne" by Percy Aldridge Grainger,
copyright © 1966 G. Schirmer, Inc. (ASCAP).

## SUGGESTED EXCERPTS

(* indicates those recommended for the beginning level conductor)

*Simple Subdivided Meters*
    Jacob: "Pavane" from *William Byrd Suite**
    Grainger: *The Sussex Mummers' Christmas Carol*
    Mozart: "Romanze" from Serenade K. 361/370a*
    Strauss: Serenade, Op. 7
    Vaughan Williams: *Rhosymedre**

*Compound Subdivided Meters*
    Burns: *The Banks O' Doon**
    Rimsky-Korsakov: *Scheherazade*, Op. 35

*Simple Asymmetrical Meters*

    Grainger: "Horkstow Grange" from *Lincolnshire Posy*

    Holst: "Mars—The Bringer of War" from *The Planets*, Op. 32*

    Mussorgsky: "Promenade" from *Pictures at an Exhibition*

    Williams: Symphonic Dance No. 3

*Changing Meters*

    Bernstein: "America" from *West Side Story**

    Bernstein: Overture to *Candide*

    Holst: "Intermezzo" from First Suite in E-flat, Op. 28, No. 1

    Holst: "The Song of the Blacksmith" from Second Suite in F,
       Op. 28, No. 2

# Unit 5
## Asymmetrical Meters

The first step in conducting fast asymmetrical meters (such as 5/8 and 7/8) is the same as when conducting divided meters: determine the standard pattern that will be used as the framework. This involves determining the number of pulses in each measure and choosing the pattern that most clearly shows these pulses. For example, an 8/8 meter calls for a 4/4 pattern if four pulses are present, but a 3/4 pattern if three pulses are evident.

In these lopsided patterns, it is important to maintain a strict mental subdivision within the larger pattern, adjusting the speed of the gesture to maintain an accurate temporal relationship between all beats and their subdivisions. The subdivision framework must never waver; only the speed of the gesture changes to accommodate the changing time of the beat.

### Two-Beat Measures

Use a two-beat pattern for 5/8 meter. Practice the following exercise using an extended gesture with constant movement for the "long" beats containing three eighth notes. Just as when conducting one beat to the bar, continue the upward movement as long as possible before giving the next beat (see Unit 2). For a more aggressive or marcato approach, move an equal distance (and speed) for both beats, creating a "stopped" beat effect.

Isolate each measure (A, B, C, and D) before conducting combinations of measures (A + B, B + C + D, etc.)

**Exercise 5.1.** Two-Beat Measures

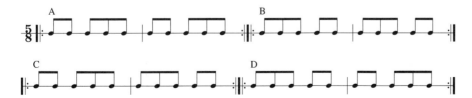

## THREE-BEAT MEASURES

**EXERCISE 5.2.** Three-Beat Measures
Use a three-beat framework for 7/8 and 8/8. Practice at various tempos with a metronome set to click eighth notes (eighth note = 160 to eighth note = 180).

## FOUR-BEAT MEASURES

**EXERCISE 5.3.** Four-Beat Measures
Use a four-beat pattern for 9/8 and 10/8.

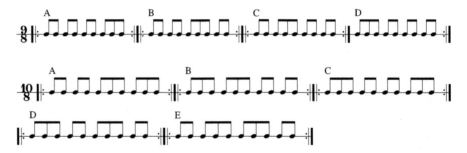

**EXERCISE 5.4.** Combined Asymmetrical Meters
These two lines combine asymmetrical meters in a way that tests both physical and mental skills. For additional practice, conduct the 7/8 bar as 2 + 3 + 2 and 2 + 2 + 3; conduct the 5/8 bar as 2 + 3.

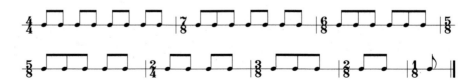

**EXERCISE 5.5.** Combined Asymmetrical Meters

Two beats for each measure:

From *Armenian Dances* by Alfred Reed, copyright © 1974 Sam Fox Publishing Company, Inc.
Used by permission. (See page 179 for full version.)

*Additional Practice*

From *Aegean Festival Overture* by Andreas Makris, copyright © 1970 Galaxy Music
Corporation. Used by permission. (See page 172 for full version.)

From *Sinfonia India* (Symphony No. 2) by Carlos Chávez, copyright © 1950 G. Schirmer,
Inc. (ASCAP). Used by permission. (See page 88 for full version.)

# SUGGESTED EXCERPTS

*Fives*

    Grainger: "Rufford Park Poachers" from *Lincolnshire Posy*

    Reed: *Armenian Dances*

*Sevens, Eights, and Nines*

    Chávez: *Sinfonia India* (Symphony No. 2)

    Makris: *Aegean Festival Overture*

# Unit 6
## Use of the Left Hand

As the novice conductor begins to learn the principles of beat patterns and how to use the baton to convey musical meaning, instruction in the independent use of the left hand should also begin. Before attempting the use of the left hand in musical context, several practice exercises should first be mastered.

## Cueing Exercise

Using standard beat patterns (two, three, and four), practice using the left hand to cue imaginary players in various places around an imaginary ensemble. First, establish a pattern. The more the novice conductor can make this pattern work on autopilot, the better. After a steady beat pattern is established, give cues on the various beats. Begin with cues on downbeats, as these are the easiest to coordinate with baton movement.

Consider the position of the fingers and the shape of left hand. The fingers should be held close together without squeezing. Fingers should never be spread. The left hand should remain in a natural cupped shape, never extended flat. Work to keep the left hand relaxed and natural in appearance.

For this cueing exercise, keep the left palm facing the floor, and indicate cues straight down, starting and ending at the ictus plane. Do not flatten the hand or use a pointing gesture.

Practice each measure separately before creating exercises using various combinations of measures. Arrows indicate cues.

**Exercise 6.1.** Cueing

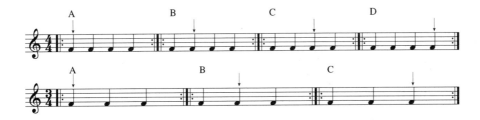

## VOLUME EXERCISE

Again, using standard patterns, establish a steady pulse. Then use the left hand to indicate a *crescendo* with an upward movement of the hand and arm, followed by a *diminuendo* with a downward movement. Begin with 4/4 meter, indicating one measure of *crescendo* followed by one measure of *diminuendo*, then repeat several times in sequence. The goal is a smooth up-and-down movement of the left hand without arm movement no matter the tempo or meter.

As in the cueing exercise, keep the fingers of the left hand together and the hand in a natural cupped shape. When moving up, turn the hand such that the index finger points to ten o'clock. When the top of the gesture is reached (no higher than the level of your eyes), turn the hand slowly and smoothly until the palm is down and then complete the downward movement. Work to integrate this hand turn into the completion of the upward motion and the start of the downward motion for one continuous movement. Start and end at the ictus plane.

Practice the following in a variety of tempos, articulations, and dynamic high and low points (e.g., *piano* to *forte*, *mezzo forte* to *fortissimo*). For additional practice, add cues on selected beats.

**EXERCISE 6.2.** Conducting dynamic changes

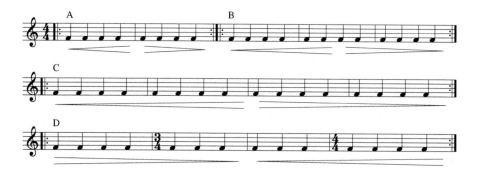

## SUSTAIN AND RELEASE EXERCISE

In addition to cues and dynamics, the indication of breaths and phrase endings can also be practiced. Use the left hand either with a slow horizontal movement or a still hand with the palm facing up to indicate a sustained note (arrow) followed by its release gesture (breath mark).

**EXERCISE 6.3.** Sustain and Release

## MIRRORING

The use of the left hand to beat time with the right is an acceptable practice when a specific musical intent is desired. Do not mirror simply so that the left hand will have something to do. This only diminishes the impact of the left hand for other purposes. A cue, *crescendo*, or release buried within a mirrored pattern will be much harder for players to pick out from the surrounding (continuous) motion. A left-hand gesture given when that hand was not previously moving has much greater impact because it will not be lost in the clutter of motion.

Mirroring *can* have musical meaning when used sparingly and carefully:

- to show the breadth of a musical line
- to show strength and impact for a particular attack or phrase point
- to show more volume by looking larger than one arm can show
- to focus player attention toward a specific point in space (especially when the mirrored pattern is smaller and close to the conductor)
- to impart more confidence to players (especially at entrances or in softer passages)

The conductor should keep in mind that mirrored patterns do not in themselves show a louder dynamic level. If the pattern is kept low, emphasizing the horizontal rather than the vertical, the result can be a soft but well supported and sustained sound.

Of course, mirroring is often used in louder passages to show increased dynamic. A particularly good use of mirroring is as the music nears the height of a *crescendo*. After a left hand indication of a *crescendo* reaches a comfortable upper limit (in relation to the height of the conductor and eye line of the players), moving into a mirrored pattern can show a continuing *crescendo* with the increased size of the pattern.

Return to Exercise 6.2 and practice with mirrored hands. In sections C and D of Exercise 6.2, use the baton hand alone to start each group at *piano*, add the left hand to mirror at the top of the *crescendo*, and then remove the left hand as the *piano* is approached again.

*Additional Practice*

Practice these exercises first without any mirroring. Use the left hand to indicate dynamic shape. Later, mirroring can be added, but be sure to consider the musical intent of mirroring at all times.

**EXERCISE 6.4.** Use of the Left Hand

From "Elsa's Procession to the Cathedral" by Richard Wagner. (See page 213 for full version.)

From *Salvation Is Created* by Pavel Tschesnokoff, copyright © 1945 Neil A. Kjos Music Company. Used by permission. (See page 194 for full version.)

From *Trauersinfonie* by Richard Wagner, copyright © 1949 (renewed) Associated Music Publishers, Inc. Used by permission. (See page 215 for full version.)

## SUGGESTED EXCERPTS

*Cues*

    Bernstein: Overture to *Candide*

    Jacob: "Pavane" from *William Byrd Suite*

    Chávez: *Sinfonia India* (Symphony No. 2)

    Holst: "Chaconne" from First Suite in E-flat, Op. 28, No. 1

    Holst: "Intermezzo" from First Suite in E-flat, Op. 28, No. 1

    Holst: "March" from First Suite in E-flat, Op. 28, No. 1

    Holst: "Song Without Words: I'll Love My Love" from Second Suite
        in F, Op. 28, No. 2

    Jacob: "Finale" from *An Original Suite*

    Reed: *Armenian Dances*

    Vaughan Williams: "My Bonnie Boy" from *English Folk Song Suite*

*Releases*

    Billings: *Chester*

    Chance: *Variations on a Korean Folk Song*

    Elgar: "Theme" from *Enigma Variations*, Op. 36

    Holst: *I Vow to Thee My Country*

*Dynamics*

    Elgar: "Theme" from *Enigma Variations*, Op. 36

    Grainger: "Horkstow Grange" from *Lincolnshire Posy*

    Holst: "Chaconne" from First Suite in E-flat, Op. 28, No. 1

    Strauss: Serenade, Op. 7

    Susato: *Ronde—Mon Amy*

    Tschesnokoff: *Salvation Is Created*

    Wagner: "Elsa's Procession to the Cathedral" from *Lohengrin*

    Wagner: *Rienzi* Overture

    Wagner: *Trauersinfonie*

# Unit 7
## Changing Dynamics
## and Tempo

### Conducting Changes in Dynamics

Conducting gradual changes in dynamics is accomplished through the use of an independent left hand effectively combined with mirroring. The conductor should work to make the use of the left hand a seamless part of conducting and as natural in appearance as possible. The subtle use of the left hand will effectively show changes in dynamics and intensity:

- moving not only up and down, but side to side and at other angles
- moving toward and away from the player
- turning the hand to show more or less palm to the player
- opening and closing the hand (moving the fingers out and in)

As security and finesse in left hand independence continue to grow, the conductor should also work toward mastering control of the baton to create beat patterns ranging from the very smallest baton-tip only movement to the largest two-arm mirrored patterns. Consistent practice of the ictus exercise from Unit 1 with various beat patterns will help the conductor gain this control. When control of beat size is combined with effective independent use of the left hand, the indication of gradual dynamic changes can be successfully accomplished

Showing sudden changes in dynamics can also be accomplished with the left hand. However, additional control of the baton is also required. As discussed in Unit 1, the beat preparation can control the dynamic level of an entrance or attack. A large preparation indicates a louder attack; a smaller preparation indicates a softer one.

Within the beat pattern, every rebound is a preparation. The rebound from beat one is the preparation for beat two, and so on. The conductor must be able to control each rebound such that it indicates the necessary information for the upcoming beat; he is free to indicate this upcoming beat after the previous ictus. Sudden changes in dynamics, then, can be shown by controlling the rebound immediately preceding the change.

- To indicate a *subito* change from *forte* to *piano* (assuming larger rebounds in *forte*), limit the size of the rebound, thus showing a small preparation for the next entrance.

- To indicate a *subito* change from *piano* to *forte* (assuming smaller rebounds in *piano*), pull the baton up from the previous ictus to show a suddenly larger preparation.

**EXERCISE 7.1.** *Subito* Dynamic Change

Arrows indicate where rebounds should change.

From *Sea Songs* by Ralph Vaughan Williams, copyright © 1924 Boosey & Co. Used by permission. (See page 198 for full version.)

From *Country Gardens* by Percy Aldridge Grainger, copyright © 1919 G. Schirmer, Inc. (ASCAP). Used by permission. (See page 92 for full version.)

## CONDUCTING TEMPO CHANGES

Indication of gradual tempo changes requires control of beat size. At the start of an *accelerando*, gradually decrease the beat size (smaller rebounds). For *ritardandos*, gradually increase the beat size (larger rebounds).

Conductors should be ready for a bit of discomfort when indicating gradual tempo changes. The ensemble may lag behind the beat at the start of accelerations, especially those that increase in speed quickly. However, the ensemble will eventually catch up, and the conductor must be willing to be ahead of the ensemble until this happens. The accelerando will not be successfully achieved if the conductor falls back to the ensemble. Similarly, ensembles will play ahead of the conductor at the start of many *ritardandos*. Maintain the desired rate of change, and the ensemble will catch up. Do not overuse subdivided beats to show *ritardandos*. Only the most *molto* of *ritardandos* require the indications of subdivisions.

Effective communication of *rubato* is accomplished by the control of rebounds and preparations. Do not hesitate to pull or push tempos by changing the time and distance between icti. To delay a beat, move away from that ictus point for the majority of the time between beats. For example, to delay beat one in 4/4 time, move upward until just before beat one; to delay beat three in 4/4 time, continue movement to the left (beat two) as long as possible. Movement toward the next beat too soon may indicate an earlier entrance to some players. When stretching beats in this manner, lead with the hand and allow the tip of the baton to drag behind.

Practice various beat patterns with combinations of *accelerandos* and *ritardandos* by establishing the three necessary parameters:

starting tempo      duration of activity      ending tempo

Return to the exercises at the end of Unit 6 for practice with rubato.

## SUBITO TEMPO CHANGES

Sudden tempo changes, such as those encountered between discreet sections of a piece of music, can be effectively controlled though the rebound and the preparation. As stated earlier, every rebound is the preparation for the following beat. The clearest tempo change preparations move in the new tempo from a stopped position. Whenever possible, follow this simple procedure:

1. Come to a stop after a slight rebound of the last pulse before the tempo change with hands in position to prepare the next beat.

2. Remain still.

3. Prepare the next beat in the new tempo, and continue in that tempo.

Of course, there will be many instances when a stop is not physically possible or musically warranted. In these cases, clear tempo changes can be achieved by focusing the performers' attention on the baton. As the tempo change is approached, move the beat pattern toward the centerline of the body. Hands wide apart do not offer the same center of focus as hands closer together.

Practice the following *subito* tempo change exercises. Be sure to establish the new tempo in your mind before attempting the change.

**EXERCISE 7.2.**

## SUGGESTED EXCERPTS

Subito *Dynamic Changes*

Bernstein: "America" from *West Side Story*

Bernstein: Overture to *Candide*

Grainger: *Country Gardens*

Holst: "March" from First Suite in E-flat, Op. 28, No. 1

Jacob: "Finale" from *An Original Suite*

Mozart: "Romanze" from Serenade K. 361/370a

Susato: *La Mourisque*

Vaughan Williams: *Sea Songs*

Vaughan Williams: "Seventeen Come Sunday"
    from *English Folk Song Suite*

*Gradual Dynamic Changes*
    Bernstein: Overture to *Candide*
    Burns: *The Banks O' Doon*
    Jacob: "Pavane" from *William Byrd Suite*
    Grainger: *Country Gardens*
    Grainger: *The Sussex Mummers' Christmas Carol*
    Holst: "Chaconne" from First Suite in E-flat, Op. 28, No. 1
    Holst: "March" from Second Suite in F, Op. 28, No. 2
    Sousa: *Manhattan Beach March*
    Strauss: Serenade, Op. 7
    Wagner: "Elsa's Procession to the Cathedral" from *Lohengrin*
    Wagner: *Trauersinfonie*

*Conducting Tempo Changes*
    Burns: *The Banks O' Doon*
    Elgar: "Theme" from *Enigma Variations*, Op. 36
    Grainger: "Horkstow Grange" from *Lincolnshire Posy*
    Grainger: *The Sussex Mummers' Christmas Carol*
    Holst: "Song Without Words: I'll Love My Love"
        from Second Suite in F, Op. 28, No. 2
    Tschesnokoff: *Salvation Is Created*
    Vaughan Williams: *Rhosymedre*
    Wagner: *Trauersinfonie*

# UNIT 8
## FROM SCORE TO PODIUM

### GETTING TO KNOW THE SCORE

The more you know what is contained in the score, the better you are able to represent the composer on the podium. You can certainly develop your own thoughts and feelings about the music, but a conductor's primary responsibility is to the composer and *his* thoughts, feelings, and intent. To this end, a conductor's goal should be to know what is printed in the score as well as if he or she had written it.

- Read and know the meaning of every printed word and marking in the score:
    - Translate all foreign terms
    - Associate a range of acceptable tempos to each tempo indication
    - Research possible interpretations for each articulation or stylistic indication
    - Look for any "user" instructions (mutes, mallets, bowings, etc.)
- Be familiar with the score layout:
    - Locate each instrument and instrument family
    - Determine if the score is transposed or in concert key
    - Locate rehearsal and section markings
- Know the transposition of each instrument

After becoming familiar with the score and its contents, go beyond the score. Investigate the origins of the work and the background of the composer. Understand the stylistic period or genre represented by the piece and its appropriate performance practice. Drawing on your knowledge of historical context, the composer's other works, musical form, and function will all inform your conducting decisions.

### DEVELOPING AN AURAL IMAGE

Each conductor must find his or her own way toward an aural image of a score. There are as many paths as there are conductors. Some conductors find it easiest to work from the top down with a macro to micro approach. Others find the opposite approach more comfortable or efficient. In either case, the conductor must become familiar with all musical elements presented:

- form, structure, and phrase construction
- meter, tempo, and rhythm
- key, harmony, and harmonic progression
- orchestration and texture
- dynamic shape
- style and performance practice (including articulation interpretation)
- technical considerations of range, rhythm, fingering, etc.

Recordings can be a useful tool, but be wary of using them as a crutch. Listening to a single recording of a work can imprint a specific musical result onto the conductor that may not accurately reflect what is in the score. There can be no substitute for first-hand study, exploration, and decision-making. The conductor should study the elements listed above to develop:

- a sense of where each phrase comes from and where it leads to through a study of form, structure, harmonic progression, and phrasing
- an internalization of each tempo presented in the piece
- an understanding of the function of each instrument (how it fits in the orchestration and texture of the piece) and how these functions change
- a relative scale of all dynamics presented
- a concept of note length, shape, and articulation (style)

## FROM AURAL IMAGE TO GESTURE

When the conductor has developed an aural image of the score he or she can create gestures to reflect what was learned about the score and its contents. As we said in Unit 2, the baton and its movement can be roughly correlated to sound. All conducting gestures should reflect the aural image. That is: *gesture represents sound.*

As gestures are developed and practiced, do not overlook the need to train your ensemble in the interpretation of these gestures. Many gestures can have a kind of universal meaning, but the more subtle gestures require some education and familiarity. Do not hesitate to use words with gesture at first. Associate musical and non-musical terms with gesture. Words such as "bold," "majestic," "hard," "floating," "timid," and "bubbly" work as well (and sometimes better) that musical terminology. Conducting with a legato gesture while verbally asking for a legato articulation will help players understand what you mean.

On the podium, the conductor must constantly monitor the effect of gestures and continually sensitize his or her players to read those gestures. The effective and efficient conductor may need to modify his or her gestures to match what he or she hears.

The conductor must not always blame the player for misreading gestures—they are what they are. If a gesture designed to look staccato appears to the players as marcato, then you may have given a marcato gesture! If a gesture devised to elicit a *forte* dynamic of a specific level produces a softer dynamic from the players, the conductor may need to make the gesture stronger (harder, larger, etc.) in order to elicit the desired response. Continual sensitization of player to gesture will help close the gap between conductor indication of gestures and player interpretation of those gestures.

The goal of the conductor should be the matching of aural image to actual music produced. "How does it sound?" should be the question each conductor asks as the rehearsal process continues. Compare your aural image with what you hear from the podium. Modifying gestures and correcting performance errors until reality matches that image are both principal elements in effective rehearsal practice.

## ON THE PODIUM

As the conductor works from the podium in rehearsals and performances, he or she should be constantly shifting the focus among three places in time: the past, present, and future. A conductor can either react to what has gone before, be in the moment of what is happening at that instant, or be proactive to illicit future responses.

Said another way:

    **evaluation:** what has just happened? (error detection)
    **activation:** what do I need to do now? (gesture)
    **anticipation:** what should I be preparing to do? (cueing; adapting)

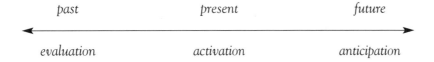

Of course, the mind cannot be in three places at once. The conductor must make a conscious decision about where to be. At the beginning of the rehearsal process, a conductor may need to spend most of his time and energy in the activation and anticipation modes simply to help the ensemble get through the music. Later in the process, the conductor may find it useful to be in evaluation mode, making decisions about what still needs to be fixed.

As you conduct, be aware of where you are. The effective conductor moves among these modes as the situation warrants but does not spend too long a period in any one mode at a stretch.

Instrumentalists who spend their musical lives reading single-line music often develop the habit of following that line as it happens in real time, rarely thinking about the past or future. If this habit is brought to score reading on the podium, the conductor will find him- or herself continually in activation mode, unable to make adjustments based on what has already happened as well as unready to prepare new or changing musical material.

Conductors who know the score well enough to function from memory may find it much easier to move from one time frame to another as the situation demands. Using your memory can force you into anticipation mode as you think ahead. You will find it easier to evaluate past musical events if you can continue to activate the continuing music from memory.

## SUGGESTED EXCERPTS

Bernstein: Overture to *Candide*

Burns: *The Banks O' Doon*

Grainger: "Horkstow Grange" from *Lincolnshire Posy*

Holst: "Chaconne" from First Suite in E-flat, Op. 28, No. 1

Holst: "March" from First Suite in E-flat, Op. 28, No. 1

Holst: "March" from Second Suite in F, Op. 28, No. 2

Holst: "Song Without Words: I'll Love My Love"
   from Second Suite in F, Op. 28, No. 2

Holst: "The Song of the Blacksmith"
   from Second Suite in F, Op. 28, No. 2

Jacob: "Finale" from *An Original Suite*

Vaughan Williams: "Seventeen Come Sunday"
   from *English Folk Song Suite*

# Unit 9
## Tools for the Conductor

### Guide to Transposition for the Conductor

Conductors should be able to read transposed parts, identifying concert or sounding pitch. Conductors should also be able write a properly transposed part, given concert pitch.

The non-transposing instruments include flute, oboe, bassoon, trumpet in C, trombone, euphonium, and tuba.

The following instruments write their parts a **major second** (or major second plus a number of octaves) **above** sounding pitch:

B-flat clarinet

B-flat bass clarinet (+ 1 octave)

B-flat contrabass clarinet
   (+ 2 octaves)

B-flat trumpet

B-flat soprano saxophone

B-flat tenor saxophone (+ 1 octave)

B-flat bass saxophone (+ 2 octaves)

B-flat baritone horn (+ 1 octave)

The following instruments write their parts a **major sixth** (or major sixth plus a number of octaves) **above** sounding pitch:

E-flat alto clarinet

E-flat contraalto clarinet
   (+ 1 octave)

E-flat alto saxophone

E-flat baritone saxophone
   (+ 1 octave)

A chart combining the clarinet and saxophone families may be of use in memorizing these common transpositions:

| Part is written up: | Clarinets | Saxophones | Brass |
|---|---|---|---|
| a major second (B-flat) | soprano | soprano | trumpet in B-flat |
| a major sixth (E-flat) | alto | alto | |
| a major second + 1 octave (B-flat) | bass | tenor | baritone (TC) |
| a major sixth + 1 octave (E-flat) | contraalto | baritone | |
| a major second + 2 octaves (B-flat) | contrabass | bass | |

**Table 9.1.** B-flat and E-flat Transpositions

Two additional members of the clarinet family are also worth noting. The clarinet in A is written a minor third **above** sounding pitch. The E-flat (soprano) clarinet is written a minor third **below** sounding pitch.

The horns write their parts a **perfect fifth above** sounding pitch:
English horn
bassethorn
French horn in F

The following instruments write their parts **one octave above** sounding pitch:
contrabassoon
string bass

The following instruments write their parts **one octave below** sounding pitch:
piccolo, chimes, xylophone, celeste
orchestra bells (two octaves below)

Only one instrument is pitched in G, the alto flute. It is written a perfect fourth **above** sounding pitch. The E-flat trumpet is written a minor third **below** sounding pitch.

In orchestral music, it is not uncommon to find trumpets and trombones pitched in a variety of key centers.

| Trumpet in: | Sounds: | Horn in: | Sounds: |
|---|---|---|---|
| A | down minor third | A | down minor third |
| B-flat | down major second | B-flat | down major second |
| C | non-transposing | C | down one octave |
| D | up major second | D | down minor seventh |
| E-flat | up minor third | E-flat | down major sixth |
| F | up perfect fourth | F | down perfect fifth |
| | | E | down minor sixth |
| | | G | down perfect fourth |
| | | B-flat basso | down a major second + 1 octave |

**TABLE 9.2.** Trumpet and Horn Transpositions

## READING CLEFS

Clefs point to middle C (𝄡), to F below middle C (𝄢), or to G above middle C (𝄞)

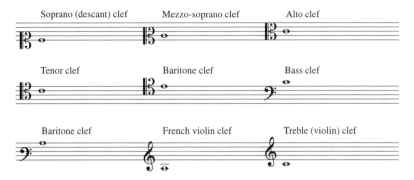

Several indispensable items should be on every conductor's desk or bookshelf:

- Metronome
- Electronic tuner
- A dictionary of musical terms and phrases
- Standard foreign language dictionaries

The metronome is invaluable during the score study process. It can help the conductor internalize pulse and tempo relationships between sections and movements of works under study. Of course, an electronic tuner is very useful in rehearsals as an aid in tuning individual pitches as well as establishing and maintaining a stable pitch center for the ensemble.

A comprehensive dictionary of musical terms should be on every conductor's bookshelf. Composers choose their terminology very carefully, and the conductor should use every means possible to understand and realize these instructions. A music dictionary might not be sufficient if a composer uses vernacular rather than standard musical terminology in his or her scores. Standard foreign language dictionaries must be consulted in these instances.

# FOREIGN INSTRUMENT NAMES IN SCORE ORDER

| English | Italian | German | French |
|---|---|---|---|
| piccolo | flauto piccolo | kleine Flöte | petite flûte |
| flute | flauto | (grosse)Flöte | flûte |
| oboe | oboe | Oboe (Hoboe) | hautbois |
| English horn | Corno Inglese | Englisch Horn | cor anglais |
| bassoon | fagotto | Fagott | basson |
| contrabassoon | contrafagotto | Kontrafagott | contre-basson |
| clarinet | clarinetto | Klarinette | clarinette |
| bass clarinet | clarinetto basso | Bassklarinette | clarinette basse |
| saxophone | sassofone | Saxophon | saxophone |
| horn | corno | Horn | cor |
| trumpet | tromba | Trompete | trompette |
| cornet | cornetto | Kornett | cornet à piston |
| flügelhorn | flicorno | Bugle | bugle |
| trombone | trombone | Posaune | trombone |
| euphonium | bariton saxhorn | Baryton | basse à pistons |
| tuba | tuba di basso | Basstuba | tuba basse |
| timpani | timpani | Pauken | timbales |
| snare drum | tamburo | kleine Trommel | casse claire, tambour |
| field drum | tamburo | Rühr trommel | tambour |
| bass drum | (gran) cassa | grosse Trommel | grosse caisse |
| cymbals | piatti | Becken | cymbales |
| triangle | triangolo | Triangel | triangle |
| tambourine | tamburino | Schnellentrommel | tambour (de Basque) |
| glockenspiel | campanelli | Glockenspiel | jeu de timbres, carillon |
| bells/chimes | campane | Glocken | cloches |
| xylophone | silofone | Sylophon | sylophone |
| marimba | marimba | Marimba | marimba |
| vibraphone | vibrafono | Vibraphon | vibraphone |
| harp | arpa | Harfe | harpe |
| violin | violino | Violine | violon |
| viola | viola | Bratsche | alto |
| violoncello | violoncello | Violoncell | violoncelle |
| double bass | contrabasso | Kontrabass | contrebasse |

**TABLE 9.3.**

# PART 2:
## EXCERPTS

# Du Lebensfürst, Herr Jesu Christ, BWV 173

J. S. Bach

# Wachet auf, ruft uns die Stimme, BVW 645

J. S. Bach

71

# Overture to Candide

Leonard Bernstein

**Allegro molto con brio**

73

# America

from *West Side Story*

Leonard Bernstein

# Chester

from *The Singing Master's Assistant* (1778)

William Billings

# The Banks O' Doon

Robert Burns

# Variations on a Korean Folk Song

John Barnes Chance

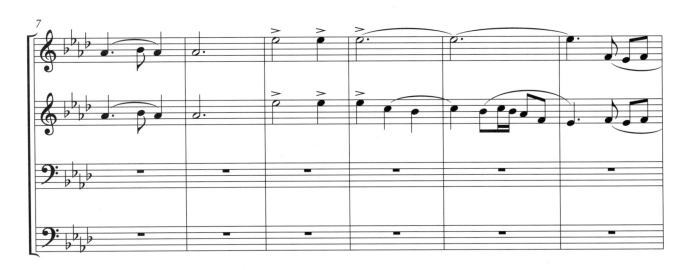

# Sinfonia India (Symphony No. 2)

Charles Chávez

# Slavonic Dances, Op. 46, No. 1

Antonín Dvořák

# Theme from Enigma Variations, Op. 36

Edward Elgar

# Country Gardens

Collected by Cecil J. Sharp
Arranged by Percy Grainger

93

# Horkstow Grange

from *Lincolnshire Posy*

Percy Aldridge Grainger

**Singingly (faster?)**

95

96

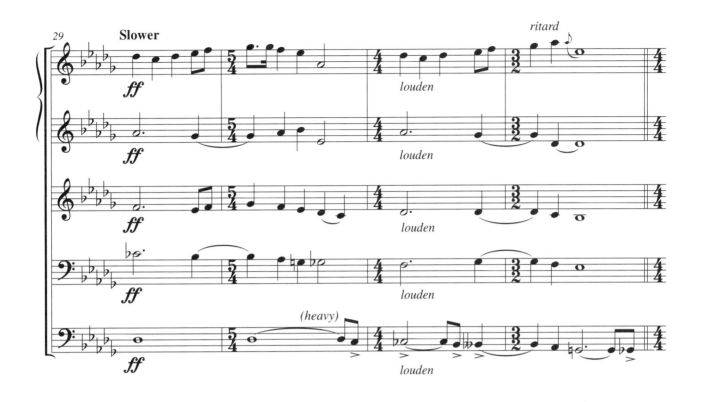

97

# Irish Tune from County Derry

Percy Aldridge Grainger

98

99

# The Lost Lady Found

from *Lincolnshire Posy*

Percy Aldridge Grainger

# Rufford Park Poachers

from *Lincolnshire Posy*

Percy Aldridge Grainger

103

# The Sussex Mummers' Christmas Carol

Percy Aldridge Grainger

# Chaconne
## from First Suite in E-flat, Op. 28, No. 1

Gustav Holst

106

**Brilliante**

115

**Maestoso**

(Cr. Cym.)

116

_rit. al fine_

# Intermezzo
## from First Suite in E-flat, Op. 28, No. 1

Gustav Holst

Triangle

Tambourine

119

Dolce (L'istesso tempo)

120

# March
## from First Suite in E-flat, Op. 28, No. 1

Gustav Holst

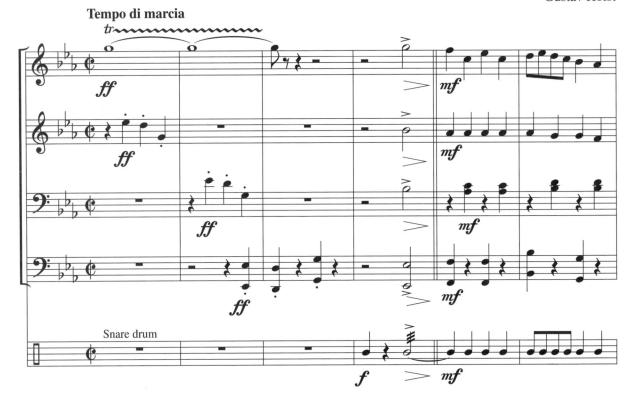

123

124

Con largezza

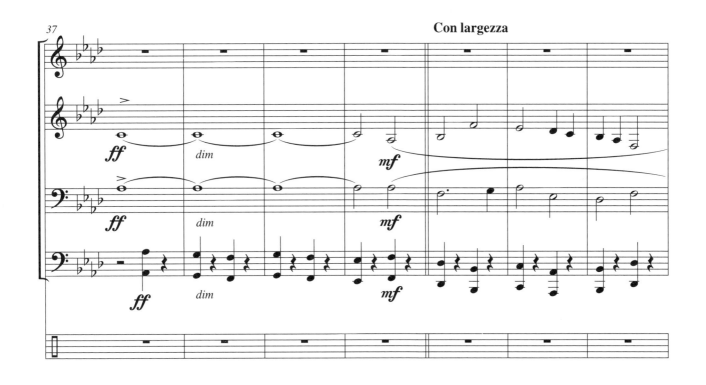

129

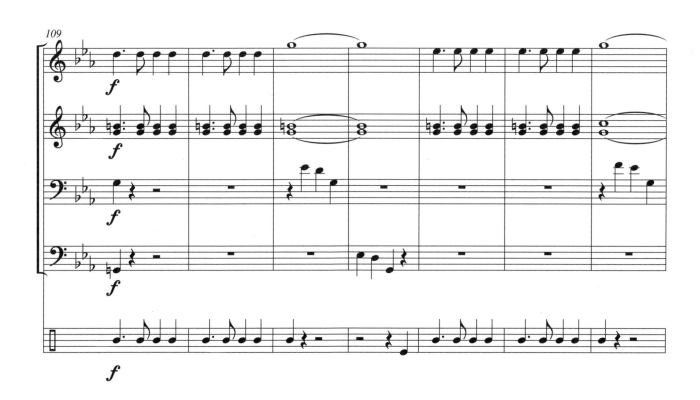

131

132

**Meno mosso**

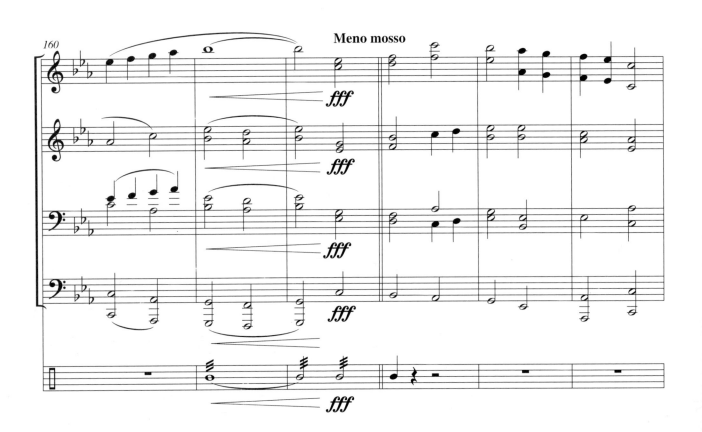

134

**Più mosso**

# March
## from Second Suite in F, Op. 28, No. 2

Gustav Holst

Cym.

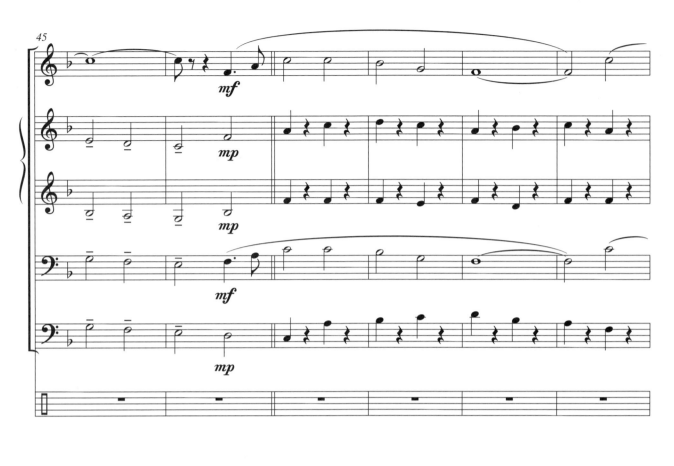

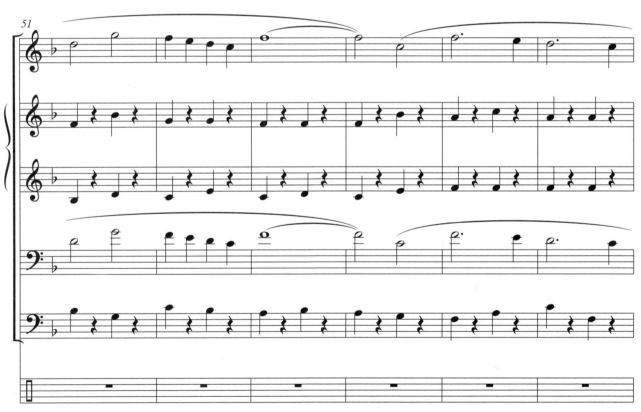

143

144

148

149

# Song Without Words: I'll Love My Love

from Second Suite in F, Op. 28, No. 2

Gustav Holst

151

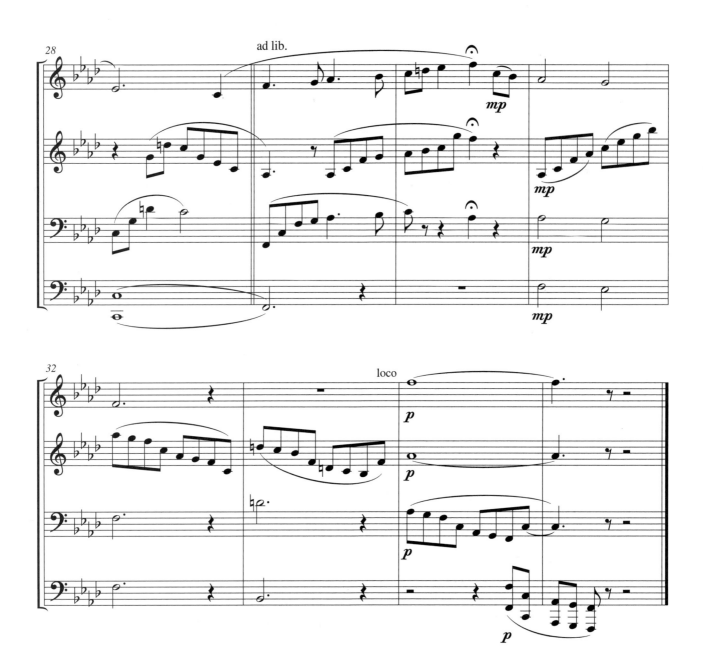

# The Song of the Blacksmith

### from Second Suite in F, Op. 28, No. 2

Gustav Holst

**Moderato e maestoso**

153

156

# I Vow to Thee My Country

Gustav Holst

# Mars—The Bringer of War

from *The Planets*, Op. 32

Gustav Holst

161

# Finale
from *An Original Suite*

Gordon Jacob

163

165

166

# Pavane
## from *William Byrd Suite*

Gordon Jacob

# Aegean Festival Overture

Andreas Makris

# Romanze
## from Serenade K. 361/370a

W. A. Mozart

175

# Promenade

from *Pictures at an Exhibition*

Modest P. Mussorgsky

# Armenian Dances

Alfred Reed

180

# Scheherazade, Op. 35

Nicholai Rimsky-Korsakov

# The Italian in Algiers—Overture

Gioachino Rossini

184

# Manhattan Beach March

John Philip Sousa

# Serenade, Op. 7

Richard Strauss

# La Mourisque

Tylman Susato

190

# Ronde—Mon Amy

Tylman Susato

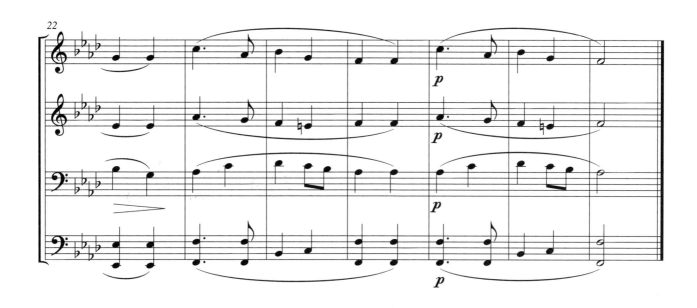

# Salvation Is Created

Pavel Tschesnokoff

# Rhosymedre

Ralph Vaughan Williams

195

196

# Sea Songs

Ralph Vaughan Williams

198

# Seventeen Come Sunday
from *English Folk Song Suite*

Ralph Vaughan Williams

to Coda ⊕

**D.C. al Coda**

208

# Green Bushes

from *English Folk Song Suite*

Ralph Vaughan Williams

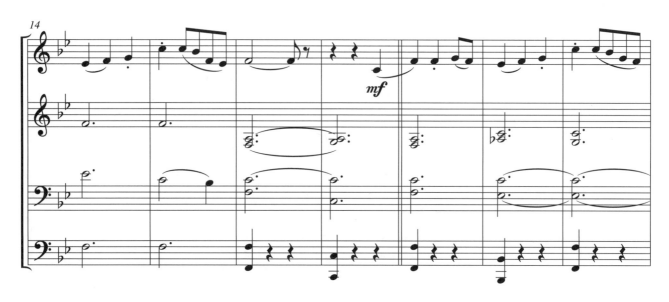

# My Bonnie Boy

from *English Folk Song Suite*

Ralph Vaughan Williams

# Elsa's Procession to the Cathedral

from *Lohengrin*

Richard Wagner

cresc poco a poco to end

cresc poco a poco to end

cresc poco a poco to end

cresc poco a poco to end

# Rienzi Overture

Richard Wagner

214

# Trauersinfonie

Richard Wagner

**Poco piu mosso**

# Symphonic Dance No. 3 "Fiesta"

J. Clifton Williams

219

# PART 3:
## INSTRUCTOR GUIDE

# Using This Text with the Beginning Conducting Class

For the beginning or introductory conducting course, the units of Part 1 are best taken in order. They present the elements of manual technique in increasing order of physical complexity. Each new skill builds on the previous. Although complete physical mastery of each unit's material cannot be expected, the student should reach a level of ease and comfort (as much as time will allow) before attempting the next unit.

The following are two suggested course outlines for the beginner's course, along with suggested excerpts from Part 2 of the text. Students should work on the exercises and examples within each chapter before using the excerpts from Part 2. Most musical examples in each chapter are also represented in the fully arranged excerpts of Part 2 and serve as a good introduction to the skills addressed in each chapter.

Each course outline can be expanded simply by adding days or weeks to each topic as time and student skill level allow. The instructor may also expand on either outline by adding classroom work on a variety of conducting-related topics that are beyond the scope of this text such as score study, error detection, rehearsal planning, and execution, all of which can be addressed using the excerpts of Part 2 as source material.

*A Ten-Week Course*

| Week | Unit | Topic | Excerpt |
|---|---|---|---|
| 1 | 1 | Posture, stance, and straight-line movement; holding the baton | |
| 2 | 1 | Ictus, preparations, downbeats, and releases | In-chapter practice exercises |
| 3 | 2 | Time beating in three | *The Italian in Algiers*; *Variations on a Korean Folk Song* |
| 4 | 2 | Time beating in four | *Salvation Is Created*; *Chester* |
| 5 | 2 | Time beating in two and one | *Sea Songs*; *Manhattan Beach*; "The Lost Lady Found"; Slavonic Dances, Op. 46, No. 1 |
| 6 | — | More practice in basic meters | Instructor/student choice *(see basic skills review in the section below)* |
| 7 | 3 | Entrances on beats other than one | *Irish Tune from County Derry*; *I Vow to Thee My Country* |
| 8 | 3 | Fermatas | Bach chorales |

| Week | Unit | Topic | Excerpt |
|------|------|-------|---------|
| 9 | 6 | Use of the left hand | In-chapter practice exercises |
| 10 | — | Culminating excerpts | Instructor/student choice |

### A Fifteen-Week Course

| Week | Unit | Topic | Excerpt |
|------|------|-------|---------|
| 1 | 1 | Posture, stance, and straight-line movement; holding the baton | |
| 2 | 1 | Ictus, preparations, downbeats, and releases | In-chapter practice exercises |
| 3 | 2 | Time beating in three | *The Italian in Algiers*; *Variations on a Korean Folk Song* |
| 4 | 2 | Time beating in four | *Salvation Is Created*; *Chester* |
| 5 | 2 | Time beating in two and one | *Sea Songs*; *Manhattan Beach*; "The Lost Lady Found"; Slavonic Dances, Op. 46, No. 1 |
| 6 | — | More practice in basic meters | Instructor/student choice (*see basic skills review below*) |
| 7 | 3 | Entrances on beats beside one | *Irish Tune from County Derry*; *I Vow to Thee My Country* |
| 8 | 3 | Fermatas | Bach chorales |
| 9 | 4 | Divided meters | "Romanze" from Serenade K. 361/370a; *Rhosymedre*; *The Banks O' Doon* |
| 10 | 4 | Simple asymmetrical meters | "Mars—The Bringer of War"; "Promenade" |
| 11 | 5 | Asymmetrical meters | In-chapter exercises; *Armenian Dances* |
| 12 | 6 | Use of the left hand | In-chapter practice exercises |
| 13 | 6 | Use of the left hand | "Elsa's Procession to the Cathedral"; *Trauersinfonie* |
| 14 | — | Culminating excerpts | Instructor/student choice |
| 15 | — | Culminating excerpts | Instructor/student choice |

## USING THIS TEXT FOR REVIEW OF BASIC SKILLS

A brief but comprehensive review of basic skills and concepts can be accommodated in a few short weeks using the units of Part 1. The material in each unit can be reviewed in a short time followed by class work on several pertinent excerpts from Part 2 as suggested below. Units 2, 3, 4, and 5 provide a review of beat patterns and will suffice as a review of the basics. The material in Units 6 and 7 may best be addressed from within the context of the intermediate course after a basic skills review is complete.

The instructor may wish to allow students their choice of one excerpt from each list or limit the choice to one or two pieces from each section. Each student may conduct more than one excerpt as time allows.

## STUDENT EVALUATION

Regular student evaluation and feedback is vital to the growth of every student. As difficult as it is to objectify the subjective art of music making, an attempt must be made. Students must know if they are making satisfactory progress in their development of physical technique. Weekly or biweekly evaluation of the following aspects of physical technique is recommended:

- **Environment, Posture, and Stance:**
    position of the music stand
    upper body posture
    stance
    ready position
    eye contact
    confidence level

- **Baton and Baton Arm:**
    Grip:     finger position
              wrist position
              baton tip position
    Hinges:   wrist
              elbow
              shoulder

- **Left Arm:**
    at-rest position
    finger position when in use
    use of mirroring
    independent use

- **Beat Patterns:**

    placement on the beat plane (use of horizontal space)

    size of beat and rebound (use of vertical space)

    clarity of pattern

    preparatory gestures

    clear ictus

    expressiveness of style

- **Musicianship:**

    has made musical decisions

    uses facial expressions

    adapts to the ensemble

    expressive use of the baton

    expressive use of the left hand

Letter or numerical grades for these facets of physical technique may not be necessary. Simply rating the student's progress is sufficient feedback during the learning process:

plus sign ( + ) to indicate excellent work or progress

check mark ( √ ) to indicate sufficient progress

minus sign ( − ) to indicate that work is needed

Sample evaluation sheets (which may be reproduced for classroom use) can be found in the appendix to this text.

## SUGGESTED EXCERPTS FOR EACH UNIT

### UNIT 2: CONDUCTING IN THREE, FOUR, TWO, AND ONE

*Time Beating in Three*

Bach: *Du Lebensfürst, Herr Jesu Christ*, BWV 173

Chance: *Variations on a Korean Folk Song*

Holst: *I Vow to Thee My Country*

Rossini: *The Italian in Algiers*

Vaughan Williams: "My Bonnie Boy" from *English Folk Song Suite*

*Time Beating in Four*

Bach: *Wachet auf, ruft uns die Stimme*, BWV 645

Billings: *Chester*

Grainger: *Country Gardens*

Grainger: *Irish Tune from County Derry*
Holst: "Song Without Words: I'll Love My Love"
   from Second Suite in F, Op. 28, No. 2
Strauss: Serenade, Op. 7

*Time Beating in Two*
Holst: "March" from First Suite in E-flat, Op. 28, No. 1
Holst: "March" from Second Suite in F, Op. 28, No. 2
Sousa: *Manhattan Beach March*
Susato: *La Mourisque*
Susato: *Ronde—Mon Amy*
Vaughan Williams: *Sea Songs*
Vaughan Williams: "Seventeen Come Sunday"
   from *English Folk Song Suite*

*Time Beating in One*
Dvořák: Slavonic Dances, Op. 46, No. 1
Grainger: "The Lost Lady Found" from *Lincolnshire Posy*
Vaughan Williams: "Green Bushes" from *English Folk Song Suite*

## Unit 3: Pick-ups, Releases, and Fermatas

*Entrances and Releases on Beats Other Than One*
Bach: *Du Lebensfürst, Herr Jesu Christ*, BWV 173
Bach: *Wachet auf, ruft uns die Stimme*, BWV 645
Chance: *Variations on a Korean Folk Song*
Grainger: *Irish Tune from County Derry*
Holst: *I Vow to Thee My Country*

*Fermatas*
Bach: *Du Lebensfürst, Herr Jesu Christ*, BWV 173
Bach: *Wachet auf, ruft uns die Stimme*, BWV 645
Grainger: *The Sussex Mummers' Christmas Carol*
Mozart: "Romanze" from Serenade K. 361/370a
Wagner: *Rienzi* Overture

## UNIT 4: DIVIDED AND CHANGING METERS

*Simple Subdivided Meters*
> Jacob: "Pavane" from *William Byrd Suite*
> Grainger: *The Sussex Mummers' Christmas Carol*
> Mozart: "Romanze" from Serenade K. 361/370a
> Strauss: Serenade, Op. 7
> Vaughan Williams: *Rhosymedre*

*Compound Subdivided Meters*
> Burns: *The Banks O' Doon*
> Rimsky-Korsakov: *Scheherazade*, Op. 35

*Simple Asymmetrical Meters*
> Grainger: "Horkstow Grange" from *Lincolnshire Posy*
> Holst: "Mars—The Bringer of War" from *The Planets*, Op. 32
> Mussorgsky: "Promenade" from *Pictures at an Exhibition*
> Williams: Symphonic Dance No. 3

*Changing Meters*
> Bernstein: "America" from *West Side Story*
> Bernstein: Overture to *Candide*
> Holst: "Intermezzo" from First Suite in E-flat, Op. 28, No. 1
> Holst: "The Song of the Blacksmith"
>    from Second Suite in F, Op. 28, No. 2

## UNIT 5: ASYMMETRICAL METERS

*Fives*
> Grainger: "Rufford Park Poachers" from *Lincolnshire Posy*
> Reed: *Armenian Dances*

*Sevens, Eights, and Nines*
> Chávez: *Sinfonia India* (Symphony No. 2)
> Makris: *Aegean Festival Overture*

## UNIT 6: USE OF THE LEFT HAND

*Cues*
> Bernstein: Overture to *Candide*
> Jacob: "Pavane" from *William Byrd Suite*

Chávez: *Sinfonia India* (Symphony No. 2)

Holst: "Chaconne" from First Suite in E-flat, Op. 28, No. 1

Holst: "Intermezzo" from First Suite in E-flat, Op. 28, No. 1

Holst: "March" from First Suite in E-flat, Op. 28, No. 1

Holst: "Song Without Words: I'll Love My Love"
    from Second Suite in F, Op. 28, No. 2

Jacob: "Finale" from *An Original Suite*

Reed: *Armenian Dances*

Vaughan Williams: "My Bonnie Boy" from *Folk Song Suite*

*Releases*

Billings: *Chester*

Chance: *Variations on a Korean Folk Song*

Elgar: "Theme" from *Enigma Variations*, Op. 36

Holst: *I Vow to Thee My Country*

*Dynamics*

Elgar: "Theme" from *Enigma Variations*, Op. 36

Grainger: "Horkstow Grange" from *Lincolnshire Posy*

Holst: "Chaconne" from First Suite in E-flat, Op. 28, No. 1

Strauss: Serenade, Op. 7

Susato: *Ronde—Mon Amy*

Tschesnokoff: *Salvation Is Created*

Wagner: "Elsa's Procession to the Cathedral" from *Lohengrin*

Wagner: *Rienzi* Overture

Wagner: *Trauersinfonie*

## UNIT 7: CHANGING DYNAMICS AND TEMPO

Subito *Dynamic Changes*

Bernstein: "America" from *West Side Story*

Bernstein: Overture to *Candide*

Grainger: *Country Gardens*

Holst: "March" from First Suite in E-flat, Op. 28, No. 1

Jacob: "Finale" from *An Original Suite*

Mozart: "Romanze" from Serenade K. 361/370a

Susato: *La Mourisque*

Vaughan Williams: *Sea Songs*

Vaughan Williams: "Seventeen Come Sunday"
    from *English Folk Song Suite*

*Gradual Dynamic Changes*
    Bernstein: Overture to *Candide*
    Burns: *The Banks O' Doon*
    Jacob: "Pavane" from *William Byrd Suite*
    Grainger: *Country Gardens*
    Grainger: *The Sussex Mummers' Christmas Carol*
    Holst: "Chaconne" from First Suite in E-flat, Op. 28, No. 1
    Holst: "March" from Second Suite in F, Op. 28, No. 2
    Sousa: *Manhattan Beach March*
    Strauss: Serenade, Op. 7
    Wagner: "Elsa's Procession to the Cathedral" from *Lohengrin*
    Wagner: *Trauersinfonie*

*Conducting Tempo Changes*
    Burns: *The Banks O' Doon*
    Elgar: "Theme" from *Enigma Variations*, Op. 36
    Grainger: "Horkstow Grange" from *Lincolnshire Posy*
    Grainger: *The Sussex Mummers' Christmas Carol*
    Holst: "Song Without Words: I'll Love My Love"
        from Second Suite in F, Op. 28, No. 2
    Tschesnokoff: *Salvation Is Created*
    Vaughan Williams: *Rhosymedre*
    Wagner: *Trauersinfonie*

## FOR THE INTERMEDIATE OR ADVANCED COURSE

While a systematic chapter-by-chapter approach is recommended for the first-semester or beginning conducting course, instructors of intermediate or advanced classes should not feel such constraints. The units of Part 1 can be used as reference material while addressing conducting topics that best suit the particular situation. As topics are presented, instructors can consult the lists above for corresponding Part 2 excerpts.

For more advanced topics, each of the excerpts of Part 2 can provide an almost unlimited combination of materials. The instructor can use any of the excerpts for instruction in aural skills and error detection. Several longer (some complete movements or pieces) excerpts have been provided, which are ideally suited for work on rehearsal techniques as well as providing the opportunity to work on several conducting challenges in a single excerpt:

| | |
|---|---|
| Leonard Bernstein: | Overture to *Candide* |
| Robert Burns: | *The Banks O' Doon* |
| Percy Aldridge Grainger: | "Horkstow Grange" from *Lincolnshire Posy* |
| Percy Aldridge Grainger: | *The Sussex Mummers' Christmas Carol* |
| Gustav Holst: | "Chaconne" from First Suite in E-flat, Op. 28, No. 1 |
| Gustav Holst: | "March" from First Suite in E-flat, Op. 28, No. 1 |
| Gustav Holst: | "March" from Second Suite in F, Op. 28, No. 2 |
| Gustav Holst: | "Song Without Words: I'll Love My Love" from Second Suite in F, Op. 28, No. 2 |
| Gustav Holst: | "The Song of the Blacksmith" from Second Suite in F, Op. 28, No. 2 |
| Gordon Jacob: | "Finale" from *An Original Suite* |
| Gordon Jacob: | "Pavane" from *William Byrd Suite* |
| Ralph Vaughan Williams: | "Seventeen Come Sunday" from *English Folk Song Suite* |

Basic skills develop as more advanced topics are presented. The instructor has only to look through the excerpts to determine their place in the content of his or her course. The following are suggested correlations for each excerpt.

## EXCERPTS ALPHABETICAL BY COMPOSER

J. S. Bach: *Du Lebensfürst, Herr Jesu Christ*, BWV 173
    *Unit 2: Conducting in Three, Four, Two, and One—Time Beating in Three*
    *Unit 3: Pick-ups, Releases, and Fermatas—Entrances and Releases*
        *on Beats Other than One*
    *Unit 3: Pick-ups, Releases, and Fermatas—Fermatas*

J. S. Bach: *Wachet auf, ruft uns die Stimme*, BWV 645
    *Unit 2: Conducting in Three, Four, Two, and One—Time Beating in Four*
    *Unit 3: Pick-ups, Releases, and Fermatas—Entrances and Releases*
        *on Beats Other than One*
    *Unit 3: Pick-ups, Releases, and Fermatas—Fermatas*

Leonard Bernstein: "America" from *West Side Story*
    *Unit 4: Divided and Changing Meters—Changing Meters*
    *Unit 7: Changing Dynamics and Tempo—Subito Dynamic Changes*

Leonard Bernstein: Overture to *Candide*
> *Unit 4: Divided and Changing Meters—Changing Meters*
> *Unit 6: Use of the Left Hand—Cues*
> *Unit 7: Changing Dynamics and Tempo—Subito Dynamic Changes*
> *Unit 7: Changing Dynamics and Tempo—Gradual Dynamic Changes*

William Billings: *Chester*
> *Unit 2: Conducting in Three, Four, Two, and One—Time Beating in Four*
> *Unit 6: Use of the Left Hand—Releases*

Gordon Jacob: "Pavane" from *William Byrd Suite*
> *Unit 4: Divided and Changing Meters—Simple Subdivided Meters*
> *Unit 6: Use of the Left Hand—Cues*
> *Unit 7: Changing Dynamics and Tempo—Gradual Dynamic Changes*

John Barnes Chance: *Variations on a Korean Folk Song*
> *Unit 2: Conducting in Three, Four, Two, and One—Time Beating in Three*
> *Unit 3: Pick-ups, Releases, and Fermatas—Entrances and Releases*
>   *on Beats Other than One*
> *Unit 6: Use of the Left Hand—Releases*

Robert Burns: *The Banks O' Doon*
> *Unit 4: Divided and Changing Meters—Compound Subdivided Meters*
> *Unit 7: Changing Dynamics and Tempo—Gradual Dynamic Changes*
> *Unit 7: Changing Dynamics and Tempo—Conducting Tempo Changes*

Carlos Chávez: *Sinfonia India* (Symphony No. 2)
> *Unit 5: Asymmetrical Meters—Sevens, Eights, and Nines*
> *Unit 6: Use of the Left Hand—Cues*

Antonín Dvořák: Slavonic Dances, Op. 46, No. 1
> *Unit 2: Conducting in Three, Four, Two, and One—Time Beating in One*

Edward Elgar: "Theme" from *Enigma Variations*, Op. 36
> *Unit 6: Use of the Left Hand—Releases*
> *Unit 6: Use of the Left Hand—Dynamics*
> *Unit 7: Changing Dynamics and Tempo—Conducting Tempo Changes*

Percy Aldridge Grainger: "Horkstow Grange" from *Lincolnshire Posy*
> *Unit 4: Divided and Changing Meters—Simple Asymmetrical Meters*
> *Unit 6: Use of the Left Hand—Dynamics*
> *Unit 7: Changing Dynamics and Tempo—Conducting Tempo Changes*

Percy Aldridge Grainger: *Irish Tune from County Derry*
    *Unit 2: Conducting in Three, Four, Two, and One—Time Beating in Four*
    *Unit 3: Pick-ups, Releases, and Fermatas—Entrances and Releases*
      *on Beats Other than One*

Percy Aldridge Grainger: "The Lost Lady Found" from *Lincolnshire Posy*
    *Unit 2: Conducting in Three, Four, Two, and One—Time Beating in One*

Percy Aldridge Grainger: "Rufford Park Poachers" from *Lincolnshire Posy*
    *Unit 5: Asymmetrical Meters—Fives*

Percy Aldridge Grainger: *The Sussex Mummers' Christmas Carol*
    *Unit 3: Pick-ups, Releases, and Fermatas—Fermatas*
    *Unit 4: Divided and Changing Meters—Simple Subdivided Meters*
    *Unit 7: Changing Dynamics and Tempo—Gradual Dynamic Changes*
    *Unit 7: Changing Dynamics and Tempo—Conducting Tempo Changes*

Gustav Holst: "Chaconne" from First Suite in E-flat, Op. 28, No. 1
    *Unit 6: Use of the Left Hand—Cues*
    *Unit 6: Use of the Left Hand—Dynamics*
    *Unit 7: Changing Dynamics and Tempo—Gradual Dynamic Changes*

Gustav Holst: "Intermezzo" from First Suite in E-flat, Op. 28, No. 1
    *Unit 4: Divided and Changing Meters—Changing Meters*
    *Unit 6: Use of the Left Hand—Cues*

Gustav Holst: "March" from First Suite in E-flat, Op. 28, No. 1
    *Unit 2: Conducting in Three, Four, Two, and One—Time Beating in Two*
    *Unit 6: Use of the Left Hand—Cues*
    *Unit 7: Changing Dynamics and Tempo—Subito Dynamic Changes*

Gustav Holst: "March" from Second Suite in F, Op. 28, No. 2
    *Unit 2: Conducting in Three, Four, Two, and One—Time Beating in Two*
    *Unit 7: Changing Dynamics and Tempo—Gradual Dynamic Changes*

Gustav Holst: "Song Without Words: I'll Love My Love"
  from Second Suite in F, Op. 28, No. 2
    *Unit 2: Conducting in Three, Four, Two, and One—Time Beating in Four*
    *Unit 6: Use of the Left Hand—Cues*
    *Unit 7: Changing Dynamics and Tempo—Conducting Tempo Changes*

Gustav Holst: "The Song of the Blacksmith"
from Second Suite in F, Op. 28, No. 2
  *Unit 4: Divided and Changing Meters—Changing Meters*

Gustav Holst: *I Vow to Thee My Country*
  *Unit 2: Conducting in Three, Four, Two, and One—Time Beating in Three*
  *Unit 3: Pick-ups, Releases, and Fermatas—Entrances and Releases*
    *on Beats Other than One*
  *Unit 6: Use of the Left Hand—Releases*

Gustav Holst: "Mars—The Bringer of War" from *The Planets*, Op. 32
  *Unit 4: Divided and Changing Meters—Simple Asymmetrical Meters*

Gordon Jacob: "Finale" from *An Original Suite*
  *Unit 6: Use of the Left Hand—Cues*
  *Unit 7: Changing Dynamics and Tempo—Subito Dynamic Changes*

Andreas Makris: *Aegean Festival Overture*
  *Unit 5: Asymmetrical Meters—Sevens, Eights, and Nines*

W. A. Mozart: "Romanze" from Serenade K. 361/370a
  *Unit 3: Pick-ups, Releases, and Fermatas—Fermatas*
  *Unit 4: Divided and Changing Meters—Simple Subdivided Meters*
  *Unit 7: Changing Dynamics and Tempo—Subito Dynamic Changes*

Modest P. Mussorgsky: "Promenade" from *Pictures at an Exhibition*
  *Unit 4: Divided and Changing Meters—Simple Asymmetrical Meters*

Alfred Reed: *Armenian Dances*
  *Unit 5: Asymmetrical Meters—Fives*
  *Unit 6: Use of the Left Hand—Cues*

Nicholai Rimsky-Korsakov: *Scheherazade*, Op. 35
  *Unit 4: Divided and Changing Meters—Compound Subdivided Meters*

Gioachino Rossini: *The Italian in Algiers*
  *Unit 2: Conducting in Three, Four, Two, and One—Time Beating in Three*

John Philip Sousa: *Manhattan Beach March*
  *Unit 2: Conducting in Three, Four, Two, and One—Time Beating in Two*
  *Unit 7: Changing Dynamics and Tempo—Gradual Dynamic Changes*

Richard Strauss: Serenade, Op. 7
    *Unit 2: Conducting in Three, Four, Two, and One—Time Beating in Four*
    *Unit 4: Divided and Changing Meters—Simple Subdivided Meters*
    *Unit 6: Use of the Left Hand—Dynamics*
    *Unit 7: Changing Dynamics and Tempo—Gradual Dynamic Changes*

Tylman Susato: *La Mourisque*
    *Unit 2: Conducting in Three, Four, Two, and One—Time Beating in Two*
    *Unit 7: Changing Dynamics and Tempo—Subito Dynamic Changes*

Tylman Susato: *Ronde—Mon Amy*
    *Unit 2: Conducting in Three, Four, Two, and One—Time Beating in Two*
    *Unit 6: Use of the Left Hand—Dynamics*

Pavel Tschesnokoff: *Salvation Is Created*
    *Unit 6: Use of the Left Hand—Dynamics*
    *Unit 7: Changing Dynamics and Tempo—Conducting Tempo Changes*

J. Clifton Williams: Symphonic Dance No. 3 "Fiesta"
    *Unit 4: Divided and Changing Meters—Simple Asymmetrical Meters*

Ralph Vaughan Williams: *Rhosymedre*
    *Unit 4: Divided and Changing Meters—Simple Subdivided Meters*
    *Unit 7: Changing Dynamics and Tempo—Conducting Tempo Changes*

Ralph Vaughan Williams: *Sea Songs*
    *Unit 2: Conducting in Three, Four, Two, and One—Time Beating in Two*
    *Unit 7: Changing Dynamics and Tempo—Subito Dynamic Changes*

Ralph Vaughan Williams: "Seventeen Come Sunday"
  from *English Folk Song Suite*
    *Unit 2: Conducting in Three, Four, Two, and One—Time Beating in Two*
    *Unit 7: Changing Dynamics and Tempo—Subito Dynamic Changes*

Ralph Vaughan Williams: "Green Bushes" from *English Folk Song Suite*
    *Unit 2: Conducting in Three, Four, Two, and One—Time Beating in One*

Ralph Vaughan Williams: "My Bonnie Boy" from *English Folk Song Suite*
    *Unit 2: Conducting in Three, Four, Two, and One—Time Beating in Three*
    *Unit 6: Use of the Left Hand—Cues*

Richard Wagner: "Elsa's Procession to the Cathedral" from *Lohengrin*
    *Unit 6: Use of the Left Hand—Dynamics*
    *Unit 7: Changing Dynamics and Tempo—Gradual Dynamic Changes*

Richard Wagner: *Rienzi* Overture
> *Unit 3: Pick-ups, Releases, and Fermatas—Fermatas*
> *Unit 6: Use of the Left Hand—Dynamics*

Richard Wagner: *Trauersinfonie*
> *Unit 6: Use of the Left Hand—Dynamics*
> *Unit 7: Changing Dynamics and Tempo—Gradual Dynamic Changes*
> *Unit 7: Changing Dynamics and Tempo—Conducting Tempo Changes*

## EXCERPTS ALPHABETICAL BY TITLE

*Aegean Festival Overture*: Andreas Makris
> *Unit 5: Asymmetrical Meters—Sevens, Eights, and Nines*

"America" from *West Side Story*: Leonard Bernstein
> *Unit 4: Divided and Changing Meters—Changing Meters*
> *Unit 7: Changing Dynamics and Tempo—Subito Dynamic Changes*

*Armenian Dances*: Alfred Reed
> *Unit 5: Asymmetrical Meters—Fives*
> *Unit 6: Use of the Left Hand—Cues*

*The Banks O' Doon*: Robert Burns
> *Unit 4: Divided and Changing Meters—Compound Subdivided Meters*
> *Unit 7: Changing Dynamics and Tempo—Gradual Dynamic Changes*
> *Unit 7: Changing Dynamics and Tempo—Conducting Tempo Changes*

Overture to *Candide*: Leonard Bernstein
> *Unit 4: Divided and Changing Meters—Changing Meters*
> *Unit 6: Use of the Left Hand—Cues*
> *Unit 7: Changing Dynamics and Tempo—Subito Dynamic Changes*
> *Unit 7: Changing Dynamics and Tempo—Gradual Dynamic Changes*

"Chaconne" from First Suite in E-flat, Op. 28, No. 1: Gustav Holst
> *Unit 6: Use of the Left Hand—Cues*
> *Unit 6: Use of the Left Hand—Dynamics*
> *Unit 7: Changing Dynamics and Tempo—Gradual Dynamic Changes*

*Chester*: William Billings
> *Unit 2: Conducting in Three, Four, Two, and One—Time Beating in Four*
> *Unit 6: Use of the Left Hand—Releases*

*Du Lebensfürst, Herr Jesu Christ*, BWV 173: J. S. Bach
    *Unit 2: Conducting in Three, Four, Two, and One—Time Beating in Three*
    *Unit 3: Pick-ups, Releases, and Fermatas—Entrances and Releases*
      *on Beats Other than One*
    *Unit 3: Pick-ups, Releases, and Fermatas—Fermatas*

"Elsa's Procession to the Cathedral" from *Lohengrin*: Richard Wagner
    *Unit 6: Use of the Left Hand—Dynamics*
    *Unit 7: Changing Dynamics and Tempo—Gradual Dynamic Changes*

"Theme" from *Enigma Variations*, Op. 36: Edward Elgar
    *Unit 6: Use of the Left Hand—Releases*
    *Unit 6: Use of the Left Hand—Dynamics*
    *Unit 7: Changing Dynamics and Tempo—Conducting Tempo Changes*

"Finale" from *An Original Suite*: Gordon Jacob
    *Unit 6: Use of the Left Hand—Cues*
    *Unit 7: Changing Dynamics and Tempo—Subito Dynamic Changes*

"Green Bushes" from *English Folk Song Suite*: Ralph Vaughan Williams
    *Unit 2: Conducting in Three, Four, Two, and One—Time Beating in One*

"Horkstow Grange" from *Lincolnshire Posy*: Percy Aldridge Grainger
    *Unit 4: Divided and Changing Meters—Simple Asymmetrical Meters*
    *Unit 6: Use of the Left Hand—Dynamics*
    *Unit 7: Changing Dynamics and Tempo—Conducting Tempo Changes*

*I Vow to Thee My Country*: Gustav Holst
    *Unit 2: Conducting in Three, Four, Two, and One—Time Beating in Three*
    *Unit 3: Pick-ups, Releases, and Fermatas—Entrances and Releases*
      *on Beats Other than One*
    *Unit 6: Use of the Left Hand—Releases*

"Intermezzo" from First Suite in E-flat, Op. 28, No. 1: Gustav Holst
    *Unit 4: Divided and Changing Meters—Changing Meters*
    *Unit 6: Use of the Left Hand—Cues*

"My Bonnie Boy" from *English Folk Song Suite*: Ralph Vaughan Williams
    *Unit 2: Conducting in Three, Four, Two, and One—Time Beating in Three*
    *Unit 6: Use of the Left Hand—Cues*

*Irish Tune from County Derry*: Percy Aldridge Grainger
    *Unit 2: Conducting in Three, Four, Two, and One—Time Beating in Four*

Unit 3: Pick-ups, Releases, and Fermatas—Entrances and Releases
on Beats Other than One

The Italian in Algiers: Gioachino Rossini
Unit 2: Conducting in Three, Four, Two, and One—Time Beating in Three

La Mourisque: Tylman Susato
Unit 2: Conducting in Three, Four, Two, and One—Time Beating in Two
Unit 7: Changing Dynamics and Tempo—Subito Dynamic Changes

"The Lost Lady Found" from Lincolnshire Posy: Percy Aldridge Grainger
Unit 2: Conducting in Three, Four, Two, and One—Time Beating in One

Manhattan Beach March: John Philip Sousa
Unit 2: Conducting in Three, Four, Two, and One—Time Beating in Two
Unit 7: Changing Dynamics and Tempo—Gradual Dynamic Changes

"March" from First Suite in E-flat, Op. 28, No. 1: Gustav Holst
Unit 2: Conducting in Three, Four, Two, and One—Time Beating in Two
Unit 6: Use of the Left Hand—Cues
Unit 7: Changing Dynamics and Tempo—Subito Dynamic Changes

"March" from Second Suite in F, Op. 28, No. 2: Gustav Holst
Unit 2: Conducting in Three, Four, Two, and One—Time Beating in Two
Unit 7: Changing Dynamics and Tempo—Gradual Dynamic Changes

"Mars—The Bringer of War" from The Planets, Op. 32: Gustav Holst
Unit 4: Divided and Changing Meters—Simple Asymmetrical Meters

"Pavane" from William Byrd Suite: Gordon Jacob
Unit 4: Divided and Changing Meters—Simple Subdivided Meters
Unit 6: Use of the Left Hand—Cues
Unit 7: Changing Dynamics and Tempo—Gradual Dynamic Changes

"Promenade" from Pictures at an Exhibition: Modest P. Mussorgsky
Unit 4: Divided and Changing Meters—Simple Asymmetrical Meters

Rhosymedre: Ralph Vaughan Williams
Unit 4: Divided and Changing Meters—Simple Subdivided Meters
Unit 7: Changing Dynamics and Tempo—Conducting Tempo Changes

Rienzi Overture: Richard Wagner
Unit 3: Pick-ups, Releases, and Fermatas—Fermatas
Unit 6: Use of the Left Hand—Dynamics

"Romanze" from Serenade K. 361/370a: W. A. Mozart
    *Unit 3: Pick-ups, Releases, and Fermatas—Fermatas*
    *Unit 4: Divided and Changing Meters—Simple Subdivided Meters*
    *Unit 7: Changing Dynamics and Tempo—Subito Dynamic Changes*

*Ronde—Mon Amy:* Tylman Susato
    *Unit 2: Conducting in Three, Four, Two, and One—Time Beating in Two*
    *Unit 6: Use of the Left Hand—Dynamics*

"Rufford Park Poachers" from *Lincolnshire Posy:* Percy Aldridge Grainger
    *Unit 5: Asymmetrical Meters—Fives*

*Salvation Is Created:* Pavel Tschesnokoff
    *Unit 6: Use of the Left Hand—Dynamics*
    *Unit 7: Changing Dynamics and Tempo—Conducting Tempo Changes*

*Scheherazade,* Op. 35: Nicholai Rimsky-Korsakov
    *Unit 4: Divided and Changing Meters—Compound Subdivided Meters*

*Sea Songs:* Ralph Vaughan Williams
    *Unit 2: Conducting in Three, Four, Two, and One—Time Beating in Two*
    *Unit 7: Changing Dynamics and Tempo—Subito Dynamic Changes*

Serenade, Op. 7: Richard Strauss
    *Unit 2: Conducting in Three, Four, Two, and One—Time Beating in Four*
    *Unit 4: Divided and Changing Meters—Simple Subdivided Meters*
    *Unit 6: Use of the Left Hand—Dynamics*
    *Unit 7: Changing Dynamics and Tempo—Gradual Dynamic Changes*

"Seventeen Come Sunday" from *English Folk Song Suite:*
Ralph Vaughan Williams
    *Unit 2: Conducting in Three, Four, Two, and One—Time Beating in Two*
    *Unit 7: Changing Dynamics and Tempo—Subito Dynamic Changes*

*Sinfonia India* (Symphony No. 2): Carlos Chávez
    *Unit 5: Asymmetrical Meters—Sevens, Eights, and Nines*
    *Unit 6: Use of the Left Hand—Cues*

Slavonic Dances, Op. 46, No. 1: Antonín Dvořák
    *Unit 2: Conducting in Three, Four, Two, and One—Time Beating in One*

"The Song of the Blacksmith"
>    from Second Suite in F, Op. 28, No. 2: Gustav Holst
>    > Unit 4: Divided and Changing Meters—Changing Meters

"Song Without Words: I'll Love My Love"
>    from Second Suite in F, Op. 28, No. 2: Gustav Holst
>    > Unit 2: Conducting in Three, Four, Two, and One—Time Beating in Four
>    > Unit 6: Use of the Left Hand—Cues
>    > Unit 7: Changing Dynamics and Tempo—Conducting Tempo Changes

The Sussex Mummers' Christmas Carol: Percy Aldridge Grainger
>    > Unit 3: Pick-ups, Releases, and Fermatas—Fermatas
>    > Unit 4: Divided and Changing Meters—Simple Subdivided Meters
>    > Unit 7: Changing Dynamics and Tempo—Gradual Dynamic Changes
>    > Unit 7: Changing Dynamics and Tempo—Conducting Tempo Changes

Symphonic Dance No. 3 "Fiesta": J. Clifton Williams
>    > Unit 4: Divided and Changing Meters—Simple Asymmetrical Meters

Trauersinfonie: Richard Wagner
>    > Unit 6: Use of the Left Hand—Dynamics
>    > Unit 7: Changing Dynamics and Tempo—Gradual Dynamic Changes
>    > Unit 7: Changing Dynamics and Tempo—Conducting Tempo Changes

Variations on a Korean Folk Song: John Barnes Chance
>    > Unit 2: Conducting in Three, Four, Two, and One—Time Beating in Three
>    > Unit 3: Pick-ups, Releases, and Fermatas—Entrances and Releases
>    >    on Beats Other than One
>    > Unit 6: Use of the Left Hand—Releases

Wachet auf, ruft uns die Stimme, BWV 645: J. S. Bach
>    > Unit 2: Conducting in Three, Four, Two, and One—Time Beating in Four
>    > Unit 3: Pick-ups, Releases, and Fermatas—Entrances and Releases
>    >    on Beats Other than One
>    > Unit 3: Pick-ups, Releases, and Fermatas—Fermatas

# APPENDIX 1:
## FORMS FOR CLASSROOM USE

# CONDUCTING EVALUATION

Name_____ Date_____

+ excellent, only minor corrections needed

√ good, some work needed

– deficiency

## BATON AND BATON ARM

_____ Wrist

_____ Elbow

_____ Shoulder

## NON-BATON ARM

_____ At-rest position

_____ Fingers

_____ Mirroring

_____ Independent motion

## BEAT PATTERNS

_____ Horizontal motion / beat plane

_____ Beat patterns

_____ Preparatory gestures

_____ Clear ictus

_____ Size of beat and rebound

## EXPRESSIVENESS

_____ Baton

_____ Left hand

_____ Facial expressions

**GRADE:**

_____

_____

_____

_____

_____

_____

_____

_____

_____

_____

_____

# CONDUCTING EVALUATION

Name_____ Date_____

+ excellent, only minor corrections needed
√ good, some work needed
– deficiency

**BEAT PATTERNS**

_____ Preparatory gestures

_____ Clear ictus

_____ Clear beat pattern

_____ Use of horizontal space

_____ Use of vertical space

**BATON-ARM HINGES**

_____ Wrist

_____ Elbow

_____ Shoulder

**NON-BATON ARM**

_____ At-rest position

_____ Fingers

_____ Independent motion

**EXPRESSIVENESS**

_____ Baton

_____ Left hand

_____ Facial expressions

**GRADE:**

_____

_____

_____

_____

_____

_____

_____

_____

_____

_____

_____

_____

# CONDUCTING EVALUATION

Name_____ Date_____

+ excellent, only minor corrections needed
√ good, some work needed
– deficiency

## ENVIRONMENT, POSTURE, AND STANCE

____ Stand position
____ Eye contact
____ Stance
____ Attention-ready position
____ Shows confidence

## BATON AND BATON ARM

*Grip:*
____ Fingers
____ Wrist
____ Baton tip

## NON-BATON ARM

____ At-rest position
____ Fingers
____ Mirroring
____ Independent motion

## BEAT PATTERNS

____ Horizontal motion / beat plane
____ Beat patterns
____ Preparatory gestures
____ Clear ictus
____ Size of beat and rebound

*Pivots:*
____ Wrist
____ Elbow
____ Shoulder

## EXPRESSIVENESS

____ Baton
____ Left hand
____ Facial expressions

**GRADE:**

_____
_____
_____
_____
_____
_____
_____
_____

# REHEARSAL OBSERVATION

Name _____  Date _____

Ensemble _____  Conductor _____

Verbal vs. non-verbal communication

Eye contact with the players

Use of the baton (clear beat patterns, musical expression, etc.)

Use of the left hand (mirroring, musical expression, etc.)

Body language and facial expressions

# APPENDIX 2:
# SUGGESTIONS FOR FURTHER READING AND STUDY

Berry, Wallace. *Form in Music*. Englewood Cliffs, NJ: Prentice Hall, 1966.

Blum, David. *The Art of Quartet Playing: The Guarneri Quartet in Conversation with David Blum*. New York: Knopf, 1986.

———. *Casals and the Art of Interpretation*. New York: Holmes & Meier, 1977.

Chesterman, Robert, ed. *Conductors in Conversation*. London: Robson, 1990.

Cook, Nicholas. *A Guide to Musical Analysis*. New York: George Braziller, 1987.

Cooper, Lynn G. *Teaching Band and Orchestra*. Chicago: GIA Publications, Inc., 2004

Copland, Aaron. *What to Listen for in Music*. Rev. ed. New York: McGraw-Hill, 1957.

Fuchs, Peter Paul. *The Psychology of Conducting*. New York: MCA Music, 1969.

Gallwey, W. Timothy. *The Inner Game of Tennis*. New York: Random House, 1974.

Green, Barry, and W. Timothy Gallwey. *The Inner Game of Music*. New York: Doubleday, 1986.

Green, Douglass M. *Form in Tonal Music*, 2nd edition. New York: Holt, Rinehart and Winston, 1979.

Green, Elizabeth A. H., and Mark Gibson. *The Modern Conductor*. 7th ed. Upper Saddle River, NJ: Pearson/Prentice-Hall, 2004.

Green, Elizabeth A. H., and Nicolai Malko. *The Conductor and His Score*. Englewood Cliffs, NJ: Prentice-Hall, 1975.

Jacob, Gordon. *How to Read a Score*. London: Hawkes and Son, 1944.

Leinsdorf, Erich. *The Composer's Advocate: A Radical Orthodoxy for Musicians*. New Haven, CT: Yale University Press, 1981.

Meyer, Leonard. *Emotion and Meaning in Music*. Chicago: University of Chicago Press, 1956.

Miles, Richard, ed. *Teaching Music through Performance in Band, Volumes 1–5*. Chicago: GIA Publications, Inc., 1997–2005.

Randel, Don, ed. *The New Harvard Dictionary of Music*. Cambridge, Mass.: Belknap Press of Harvard University Press, 1986

Rudolf, Max. *The Grammar of Conducting: A Comprehensive Guide to Baton Technique and Interpretation*. 3rd ed. New York: Schirmer Books, 1994.

Schuller, Gunther. *The Compleat Conductor*. New York: Oxford University Press, 1997.

Walter, Bruno. *Of Music and Music-Making*. Trans. by Paul Hamburger. New York: W. W. Norton, 1961.

Williamson, John E., and Kenneth L. Neidig, eds. *Rehearsing the Band*. Cloudcraft, NM: Neidig Services, 1998.

# APPENDIX 3:
# EXCERPTS CORRELATED TO TEACHING MUSIC THROUGH PERFORMANCE IN BAND SERIES

*Volume 1*

Overture to *Candide*: Leonard Bernstein (arr. Clare Grundman)

"Pavane" from *William Byrd Suite*: Gordon Jacob

*Variations on a Korean Folk Song*: John Barnes Chance

*Lincolnshire Posy*: Percy Aldridge Grainger

    "Rufford Park Poachers"

    "Horkstow Grange"

    "The Lost Lady Found"

*Irish Tune from County Derry*: Percy Aldridge Grainger

First Suite in E-flat, Op. 28, No. 1: Gustav Holst

    "Chaconne"

    "Intermezzo"

    "March"

Second Suite in F, Op. 28, No. 2: Gustav Holst

    "March"

    "Song Without Words: I'll Love My Love"

    "The Song of the Blacksmith"

*Armenian Dances*: Alfred Reed

English Folk Song Suite: Ralph Vaughan Williams

    "Seventeen Come Sunday"

    "My Bonnie Boy"

    "Green Bushes"

*Trauersinfonie* (*Trauermusik*): Richard Wagner (arr. Michael Votta / John Boyd)

*Volume 2*

*Rhosymedre*: Ralph Vaughan Williams (arr. Walter Beeler)

*Sea Songs*: Ralph Vaughan Williams

*Volume 3*

"Finale" from *An Original Suite*: Gordon Jacob

*Volume 4*

*The Sussex Mummers' Christmas Carol*: Percy Aldridge Grainger (arr. Richard F. Goldman)

*Aegean Festival Overture*: Andreas Makris

*Salvation Is Created*: Pavel Tschesnokoff (arr. Bruce Houseknecht)

"Elsa's Procession to the Cathedral" from *Lohengrin*: Richard Wagner (arr. Glenn Lucien Calliet)

Symphonic Dance No. 3 "Fiesta": J. Clifton Williams

# GLOSSARY

**activation:** the process of indicating what is happening at the current moment in time

**anticipation:** the process of preparing what will occur in the future

**asymmetrical meter:** a meter in which the beat pattern does not indicate an equal number of beats on either side of the *centerline* OR a meter which does not have an equal number of subdivisions within each beat

**aural image:** the mental representation of sound

**caesura fermata:** a fermata in which the sustaining gesture comes to a complete stop using a *release gesture*

**centerline:** an imaginary vertical line dividing the body or beat pattern into equal parts

**click:** the start of the *preparation* gesture in which the wrist moves slightly downward from the *ictus plane* and then quickly upward

**communication line:** the imaginary line drawn between the eyes of conductors and players

**compound divided meter:** meters in which pulses are subdivided into three or more pulses

**downbeat:** the first pulse given, usually meant to indicate beat one

**emphatic release:** a circular *gesture* that shows players when to release the sound

**evaluation:** the process of determining what has occurred in the past

**flick:** a baton movement made by a quick movement of the wrist

**focal plane pattern:** beat patterns that place all *icti* along a horizontal plane in space

**focal point pattern:** beat patterns that place all *icti* at the same point in space

**gesture:** any physical motion, especially those made with arms, hands, and baton

**hinge:** the moving parts of the arm and hand (shoulder, elbow, wrist)

**ictus (point):** the physical indication of the beat or pulse (*pl.* icti)

**ictus plane:** the horizontal line on which an *ictus* is made

**in-time fermata:** a fermata in which the *release gesture* moves directly into the preparation of the next entrance

**mirror(ing):** the use of both hands and/or arms to show only the beat pattern

**no-release fermata:** a fermata in which there is no *release gesture*; the sustaining gesture moves directly into the *preparation* gesture

**orchestration:** the instruments used in a work and their function (melody, bass line, etc.)

**pattern symmetry:** maintaining equal size *gestures* on both sides of the *centerline*

**preparation:** the *gesture* before the *ictus*

**push-off:** the start of the *preparation* gesture in which the arm moves slightly downward from the *ictus plane* and then quickly upward

**ready position:** the position of body, arms, hands and baton indicating the readiness of the conductor to start

**rebound:** an upward *gesture* following an *ictus*

**release gesture:** the movement, including its *preparation*, intended to show the player(s) when to stop the sound

**simple divided meter:** meters in which pulses are subdivided into two pulses

**stopped beat:** halting the motion within a beat pattern after an ictus

**supermetric pattern:** a beat pattern encompassing more than one pulse

**texture:** a description of the number of voices or parts sounding at the same time in a work

# ABOUT THE AUTHOR

Douglas Stotter has taught conducting for twenty years. He is currently Director of Bands, Associate Professor of Music, and Coordinator of Winds and Percussion at the University of Texas Arlington. There, he conducts the wind ensemble and teaches undergraduate and graduate conducting and wind literature courses while overseeing all aspects of the band program.

Stotter taught previously at Indiana University, where he conducted the concert and symphonic bands and taught advanced undergraduate and graduate instrumental conducting courses. He has also served as Director of Bands at Valdosta State University, the University of Missouri–Rolla, Doane College, and Galesburg (Illinois) High School.

Stotter received bachelor's and master's degrees in music education from the University of Michigan, where his undergraduate conducting teachers included Elizabeth A. H. Green. He received the doctor of musical arts degree from the University of Iowa, where he studied with Myron Welch.

Stotter's other publications include contributions to *Teaching Music through Performance in Band* (GIA) as well as research into the history of Edwin Franko Goldman and the Goldman Band, which was published in the *Journal of Band Research*. His arrangement of songs by Ralph Vaughan Williams, *Three Dorset Songs*, was published in 2003 by Daehn Music.